50 High-Fat Food Recipes for Home

By: Kelly Johnson

Table of Contents

- Classic Bacon Cheeseburger
- Loaded Baked Potato with Sour Cream and Bacon
- Avocado Toast with Poached Egg
- Keto Cauliflower Mac and Cheese
- Butter Chicken (Murgh Makhani)
- Cheese and Spinach Stuffed Chicken Breast
- Alfredo Pasta with Parmesan and Cream
- Creamy Mushroom Risotto
- Bacon-Wrapped Jalapeno Poppers
- Pork Belly Bites with BBQ Sauce
- Beef Stroganoff with Sour Cream
- Salmon with Garlic Butter Sauce
- Cheese Fondue with Bread and Vegetables
- Hollandaise Sauce with Asparagus
- Chicken Alfredo Pizza with Extra Cheese
- Creamy Shrimp Scampi Pasta
- Loaded Cheese Fries with Bacon
- Cheesecake with Raspberry Sauce
- Buttered Lobster Tails
- Creamy Tomato Basil Soup with Heavy Cream
- Avocado and Bacon Stuffed Mushrooms
- Chocolate Peanut Butter Fat Bombs
- Creamy Spinach Artichoke Dip
- Coconut Milk Curry with Chicken
- Mascarpone-Stuffed Strawberries
- Garlic Parmesan Wings
- Creamy Parmesan Polenta
- Pecan Pie with Whipped Cream
- Blue Cheese and Bacon Burger
- Loaded Nachos with Guacamole and Sour Cream
- Bacon-Wrapped Scallops
- Creamy Carbonara Pasta
- Keto Fathead Pizza with Pepperoni and Cheese
- Cheesy Garlic Bread
- Creamy Peanut Butter Fudge
- Cream Cheese Stuffed Bell Peppers

- Bacon-Wrapped Filet Mignon
- Cheesy Broccoli Casserole
- Buttered Popcorn with Sea Salt
- Keto Cheese Crackers
- Creamy Avocado Soup with Bacon
- Cheesy Mashed Potatoes
- Creamy Caesar Salad with Bacon Bits
- Buttered Corn on the Cob
- Keto Chocolate Mousse
- Brie and Bacon Stuffed Chicken Thighs
- Creamy Coleslaw with Mayonnaise
- Cheesesteak Stuffed Peppers
- Creamy Pumpkin Soup with Coconut Milk
- Keto Cheesecake Fat Bombs

Classic Bacon Cheeseburger

Ingredients:

- 1 lb ground beef (preferably 80% lean)
- Salt and pepper, to taste
- 4 slices cheddar cheese
- 4 hamburger buns
- 8 slices bacon, cooked until crispy
- Lettuce leaves
- Sliced tomatoes
- Sliced red onion
- Pickles (optional)
- Ketchup, mustard, mayonnaise (optional, for topping)

Instructions:

1. **Form the patties:**
   - Divide the ground beef into 4 equal portions. Shape each portion into a patty about 1/2-inch thick. Press a slight indentation into the center of each patty to prevent it from puffing up while cooking. Season both sides generously with salt and pepper.
2. **Cook the patties:**
   - Heat a grill or skillet over medium-high heat. Cook the patties for about 4-5 minutes per side, or until they reach your desired level of doneness (medium-rare to well-done). During the last minute of cooking, place a slice of cheddar cheese on each patty to melt.
3. **Prepare the buns:**
   - While the patties are cooking, toast the hamburger buns lightly on the grill or in a toaster.
4. **Assemble the burgers:**
   - Place a cooked patty with melted cheese on the bottom half of each toasted bun.
   - Top each patty with 2 slices of crispy bacon.
   - Add lettuce leaves, sliced tomatoes, sliced red onion, and pickles (if using).
5. **Add condiments (optional):**
   - Spread ketchup, mustard, and/or mayonnaise on the top half of the bun, if desired.
6. **Serve:**
   - Place the top half of the bun on top of the burger to complete the sandwich. Serve the Bacon Cheeseburgers immediately while hot.

Tips:

- **Cheese variation:** You can use other types of cheese such as American cheese, Swiss cheese, or pepper jack cheese for a different flavor profile.

- **Bacon preparation:** Cook the bacon until crispy for added texture and flavor in the burger.
- **Customization:** Feel free to customize your burger with additional toppings like avocado slices, caramelized onions, or a fried egg for a gourmet twist.

This classic Bacon Cheeseburger recipe is perfect for a satisfying meal any time of the year, whether you're grilling outdoors or cooking indoors on the stove. Enjoy the delicious combination of savory beef, melted cheese, crispy bacon, and fresh toppings!

Loaded Baked Potato with Sour Cream and Bacon

Ingredients:

- 4 large russet potatoes
- Olive oil
- Salt and pepper, to taste
- 8 slices bacon, cooked until crispy and crumbled
- 1 cup shredded cheddar cheese
- 1/2 cup sour cream
- 2 green onions, thinly sliced
- Butter, optional

Instructions:

1. **Preheat the oven:** Preheat your oven to 400°F (200°C).
2. **Prepare the potatoes:** Scrub the potatoes clean and pat them dry with paper towels. Pierce each potato several times with a fork to allow steam to escape during baking.
3. **Season and bake:** Rub each potato with olive oil and sprinkle with salt and pepper. Place the potatoes directly on the oven rack and bake for 45-60 minutes, or until tender when pierced with a fork. Cooking time will depend on the size and thickness of the potatoes.
4. **Cook the bacon:** While the potatoes are baking, cook the bacon slices in a skillet over medium heat until crispy. Transfer the cooked bacon to a paper towel-lined plate to drain excess grease. Once cooled, crumble or chop the bacon into small pieces.
5. **Prepare the toppings:** Slice the green onions thinly. Shred the cheddar cheese if not already shredded.
6. **Assemble the loaded baked potatoes:**
   - Once the potatoes are baked and tender, remove them from the oven. Carefully slice each potato lengthwise down the center, being careful not to cut all the way through.
   - Use a fork to fluff the insides of each potato. If desired, add a small pat of butter to each potato and allow it to melt.
7. **Add toppings:**
   - Sprinkle each potato generously with shredded cheddar cheese.
   - Top with a dollop of sour cream on each potato.
   - Sprinkle the crumbled bacon pieces over the sour cream.
   - Garnish with sliced green onions.
8. **Serve:** Serve the loaded baked potatoes immediately while hot.

Tips:

- **Variations:** Feel free to customize your loaded baked potatoes with additional toppings such as diced avocado, chopped fresh herbs (like parsley or chives), or a drizzle of barbecue sauce.

- **Make ahead:** You can bake the potatoes ahead of time and reheat them in the oven or microwave before adding the toppings.
- **Side dish or main course:** Loaded baked potatoes can be served as a hearty side dish alongside grilled meats or as a satisfying main course with a side salad.

This recipe for loaded baked potatoes with sour cream and bacon is sure to be a hit with its combination of creamy, cheesy, and crispy flavors. Enjoy this comforting dish for a delicious meal!

Avocado Toast with Poached Egg

Ingredients:

- 2 slices of your favorite bread (such as whole grain, sourdough, or ciabatta)
- 1 ripe avocado
- 2 large eggs
- Salt and pepper, to taste
- Red pepper flakes (optional, for garnish)
- Fresh herbs (such as cilantro or parsley), chopped (optional, for garnish)
- Lemon wedges (optional, for serving)

Instructions:

1. **Prepare the avocado:**
    - Cut the avocado in half lengthwise. Remove the pit and scoop out the flesh into a bowl. Mash the avocado with a fork until smooth or leave it slightly chunky, according to your preference. Season with salt and pepper to taste.
2. **Toast the bread:**
    - Toast the slices of bread until golden and crispy. You can use a toaster or toast them in a skillet with a little olive oil or butter for extra flavor.
3. **Poach the eggs:**
    - Fill a medium-sized saucepan with water and bring it to a gentle simmer over medium heat. Add a splash of vinegar (optional, helps the eggs hold their shape).
    - Crack each egg into a small bowl or ramekin. Using a spoon, create a gentle whirlpool in the simmering water. Carefully slide the eggs, one at a time, into the center of the whirlpool. Cook the eggs for about 3-4 minutes, or until the whites are set but the yolks are still runny. Use a slotted spoon to remove the poached eggs and place them on a paper towel-lined plate to drain excess water.
4. **Assemble the avocado toast:**
    - Spread a generous amount of mashed avocado onto each slice of toasted bread.
    - Carefully place a poached egg on top of each slice of avocado toast.
    - Season the poached eggs with a sprinkle of salt, pepper, and red pepper flakes (if using).
    - Garnish with chopped fresh herbs (if using) and serve immediately while the eggs are still warm.
5. **Serve:**
    - Optionally, serve the avocado toast with poached eggs with a wedge of lemon on the side for squeezing over the eggs.

Tips:

- **Variations:** You can customize your avocado toast with additional toppings such as sliced cherry tomatoes, crumbled feta cheese, smoked salmon, or a drizzle of hot sauce.

- **Avocado texture:** Adjust the texture of the mashed avocado to your liking – some prefer it smooth, while others enjoy it chunky with visible pieces of avocado.
- **Make it a meal:** Serve avocado toast with poached egg alongside a fresh green salad or fruit for a balanced and satisfying meal.

Avocado toast with poached egg is a popular and nutritious dish that's quick to prepare and perfect for any time of the day. Enjoy the creamy avocado, runny egg yolk, and crunchy toast combination for a delightful meal!

Keto Cauliflower Mac and Cheese

Ingredients:

- 1 large head of cauliflower, cut into florets
- 1 cup heavy cream
- 2 cups shredded cheddar cheese
- 1/2 cup grated Parmesan cheese
- 2 cloves garlic, minced
- 2 tablespoons cream cheese
- 1 teaspoon Dijon mustard (optional)
- Salt and pepper, to taste
- Fresh parsley, chopped (optional, for garnish)
- Crispy bacon bits (optional, for topping)

Instructions:

1. **Preheat the oven:** Preheat your oven to 375°F (190°C).
2. **Steam the cauliflower:** Place the cauliflower florets in a large microwave-safe bowl with a splash of water. Cover with a damp paper towel and microwave on high for 5-7 minutes, or until the cauliflower is tender. Drain well and set aside.
3. **Make the cheese sauce:**
    - In a medium saucepan, heat the heavy cream over medium heat until it starts to simmer.
    - Stir in the minced garlic and cook for 1 minute until fragrant.
    - Reduce the heat to low and gradually stir in the shredded cheddar cheese and grated Parmesan cheese until melted and smooth.
    - Add the cream cheese and Dijon mustard (if using), stirring until the cream cheese is fully incorporated and the sauce is creamy. Season with salt and pepper to taste.
4. **Combine the cauliflower and cheese sauce:**
    - Add the steamed cauliflower to the cheese sauce, gently folding until all of the cauliflower florets are coated evenly.
5. **Bake the cauliflower mac and cheese:**
    - Transfer the cauliflower and cheese mixture to a baking dish or a cast-iron skillet.
    - Sprinkle additional shredded cheddar cheese on top if desired.
    - Bake in the preheated oven for 15-20 minutes, or until the cheese is bubbly and golden brown on top.
6. **Serve:**
    - Remove from the oven and let it cool slightly before serving.
    - Garnish with chopped parsley and crispy bacon bits (if using) before serving, if desired.

Tips:

- **Variations:** You can customize your Keto Cauliflower Mac and Cheese by adding cooked bacon, diced ham, or chopped broccoli florets for added texture and flavor.
- **Storage:** Store any leftovers in an airtight container in the refrigerator for up to 3 days. Reheat in the microwave or oven until heated through.
- **Nutritional information:** This dish is keto-friendly and low in carbohydrates, making it suitable for those following a ketogenic diet.

This Keto Cauliflower Mac and Cheese recipe offers a creamy and cheesy alternative to traditional macaroni and cheese, perfect for anyone looking to reduce their carb intake while still enjoying a comforting and flavorful dish.

Butter Chicken (Murgh Makhani)

Ingredients:

- 1 lb boneless, skinless chicken thighs or breasts, cut into bite-sized pieces
- 1 cup plain yogurt
- 1 tablespoon ginger garlic paste (or minced ginger and garlic)
- 1 teaspoon ground turmeric
- 1 teaspoon ground cumin
- 1 teaspoon ground coriander
- 1/2 teaspoon red chili powder (adjust to taste)
- Salt, to taste
- 2 tablespoons ghee or butter
- 1 onion, finely chopped
- 2 tomatoes, pureed
- 1/4 cup tomato paste
- 1 tablespoon kasuri methi (dried fenugreek leaves)
- 1/2 cup heavy cream or coconut cream
- 1 tablespoon honey or sugar (optional, to balance acidity)
- Fresh cilantro, chopped (for garnish)

For the marinade:

1. In a bowl, combine yogurt, ginger garlic paste, turmeric, cumin, coriander, red chili powder, and salt. Mix well.
2. Add the chicken pieces to the marinade, ensuring they are well coated. Cover and refrigerate for at least 1 hour, or overnight for best results.

Instructions:

1. **Cook the marinated chicken:**
   - Heat 1 tablespoon of ghee or butter in a large skillet or pan over medium-high heat.
   - Add the marinated chicken pieces (reserve the marinade) and cook until they are browned and cooked through, about 7-8 minutes. Remove the chicken from the skillet and set aside.
2. **Prepare the sauce:**
   - In the same skillet, add another tablespoon of ghee or butter if needed. Add chopped onions and sauté until they become translucent and soft, about 5-6 minutes.
   - Stir in the tomato puree and tomato paste. Cook for another 5-6 minutes, stirring occasionally, until the sauce thickens and the raw smell disappears.
   - Add the reserved marinade to the skillet, along with kasuri methi (crush it between your palms before adding), and cook for 2-3 minutes.
3. **Finish the dish:**

- Reduce the heat to low. Stir in the heavy cream or coconut cream, honey or sugar (if using), and cooked chicken pieces. Simmer for another 5-7 minutes, stirring occasionally, until the sauce thickens and the chicken is heated through.
- Taste and adjust salt and spice levels if needed.

4. **Serve:**
   - Garnish with fresh chopped cilantro before serving.
   - Butter Chicken is traditionally served with naan bread or steamed rice.

Tips:

- **Marinating the chicken:** Marinating the chicken in yogurt and spices helps tenderize the meat and infuses it with flavor.
- **Adjusting spice level:** You can adjust the amount of red chili powder to suit your spice preference. For a milder dish, reduce or omit the chili powder.
- **Make it ahead:** Butter Chicken tastes even better the next day as the flavors continue to develop. It can be stored in the refrigerator for up to 3 days.

Butter Chicken (Murgh Makhani) is a rich and creamy dish that's loved for its comforting flavors. Enjoy making this classic Indian dish at home for a delicious meal!

Cheese and Spinach Stuffed Chicken Breast

Ingredients:

- 4 boneless, skinless chicken breasts
- Salt and pepper, to taste
- 1 cup fresh spinach, chopped
- 1 cup shredded mozzarella cheese (or any melting cheese of your choice)
- 1/2 cup grated Parmesan cheese
- 1/4 cup cream cheese
- 2 cloves garlic, minced
- 1 teaspoon Italian seasoning (or dried herbs of your choice)
- 1 tablespoon olive oil
- Toothpicks or kitchen twine (optional, for securing the chicken)

Instructions:

1. **Prepare the chicken breasts:**
   - Preheat your oven to 375°F (190°C).
   - Use a sharp knife to carefully butterfly each chicken breast. Lay them flat and season both sides with salt and pepper.
2. **Make the stuffing:**
   - In a mixing bowl, combine chopped spinach, mozzarella cheese, Parmesan cheese, cream cheese, minced garlic, and Italian seasoning. Mix until well combined.
3. **Stuff the chicken breasts:**
   - Spoon the spinach and cheese mixture evenly onto one side of each butterflied chicken breast.
   - Fold the other half of the chicken breast over the stuffing to enclose it. Secure the edges with toothpicks or tie with kitchen twine, if needed, to keep the filling inside.
4. **Sear the chicken:**
   - Heat olive oil in an oven-safe skillet over medium-high heat. Once hot, add the stuffed chicken breasts to the skillet.
   - Sear the chicken for 2-3 minutes on each side, or until golden brown.
5. **Bake the chicken:**
   - Transfer the skillet to the preheated oven and bake for 20-25 minutes, or until the chicken is cooked through (internal temperature should reach 165°F or 74°C).
6. **Serve:**
   - Remove the chicken from the oven and let it rest for a few minutes before serving.
   - Optionally, garnish with fresh herbs like parsley or basil before serving.

Tips:

- **Variations:** Feel free to customize the stuffing with different cheeses such as cheddar or goat cheese, and add additional ingredients like sun-dried tomatoes or mushrooms for extra flavor.
- **Side dishes:** Serve the cheese and spinach stuffed chicken breast with a side of roasted vegetables, mashed potatoes, or a fresh salad for a complete meal.
- **Make ahead:** You can prepare the stuffed chicken breasts up to the point of baking and refrigerate them for a few hours before cooking. This can help save time when preparing for a meal.

Cheese and spinach stuffed chicken breast is a delightful dish that's sure to impress with its gooey cheese filling and tender chicken. Enjoy making this flavorful recipe for a special dinner at home!

Alfredo Pasta with Parmesan and Cream

Ingredients:

- 1 lb fettuccine pasta (or any pasta of your choice)
- 1/2 cup unsalted butter
- 1 cup heavy cream
- 1 cup grated Parmesan cheese, plus extra for serving
- Salt and freshly ground black pepper, to taste
- Fresh parsley, chopped (for garnish, optional)

Instructions:

1. **Cook the pasta:**
   - Bring a large pot of salted water to a boil. Cook the pasta according to the package instructions until al dente. Reserve about 1 cup of pasta cooking water before draining.
2. **Prepare the sauce:**
   - In a large skillet or saucepan, melt the butter over medium heat.
   - Pour in the heavy cream and bring to a simmer, stirring occasionally.
   - Gradually add the grated Parmesan cheese, stirring continuously until the cheese is melted and the sauce is smooth and creamy. If the sauce is too thick, you can thin it out with a splash of reserved pasta cooking water.
3. **Combine pasta and sauce:**
   - Add the cooked and drained pasta to the skillet with the Alfredo sauce. Toss well to coat the pasta evenly with the sauce.
   - Season with salt and freshly ground black pepper to taste.
4. **Serve:**
   - Divide the Alfredo pasta among serving plates or bowls.
   - Sprinkle with additional grated Parmesan cheese and chopped fresh parsley for garnish, if desired.
   - Serve immediately while hot.

Tips:

- **Variations:** You can add grilled chicken, shrimp, or vegetables such as broccoli or peas to make it a complete meal.
- **Creaminess:** Adjust the consistency of the sauce by adding more cream or pasta cooking water as needed to achieve your desired thickness.
- **Storage:** Alfredo pasta is best served fresh, but leftovers can be stored in an airtight container in the refrigerator for up to 2 days. Reheat gently on the stove with a splash of cream or milk to revive the sauce.

Alfredo Pasta with Parmesan and Cream is a comforting and decadent dish that's perfect for a special occasion or a cozy dinner at home. Enjoy the creamy goodness of this classic Italian dish!

Creamy Mushroom Risotto

Ingredients:

- 1 ½ cups Arborio rice (or any short-grain rice suitable for risotto)
- 4 cups chicken or vegetable broth (warmed)
- 1 cup dry white wine (optional)
- 2 tablespoons unsalted butter
- 2 tablespoons olive oil
- 1 small onion, finely chopped
- 2 cloves garlic, minced
- 10 oz (about 300g) mushrooms (such as cremini, button, or wild mushrooms), sliced
- 1/2 cup grated Parmesan cheese
- 1/4 cup heavy cream
- Salt and pepper, to taste
- Fresh parsley, chopped (for garnish, optional)

Instructions:

1. **Prepare the mushrooms:**
   - In a large skillet or frying pan, heat 1 tablespoon of olive oil over medium-high heat.
   - Add the sliced mushrooms and cook until they are golden brown and caramelized, about 5-7 minutes. Season with salt and pepper to taste. Remove the mushrooms from the pan and set aside.
2. **Make the risotto:**
   - In a large saucepan or Dutch oven, heat the remaining 1 tablespoon of olive oil and 1 tablespoon of butter over medium heat.
   - Add the chopped onion and cook until softened and translucent, about 3-4 minutes.
   - Stir in the minced garlic and cook for another 1-2 minutes until fragrant.
3. **Toast the rice:**
   - Add the Arborio rice to the pan with the onions and garlic. Cook, stirring frequently, for 1-2 minutes until the rice becomes translucent around the edges.
4. **Deglaze with wine (optional):**
   - Pour in the white wine and stir constantly until it is absorbed by the rice.
5. **Cook the risotto:**
   - Begin adding the warm chicken or vegetable broth to the rice, one ladleful (about 1/2 cup) at a time.
   - Stir frequently and allow each addition of broth to be absorbed by the rice before adding more. This process will take about 18-20 minutes until the rice is tender and creamy but still slightly firm to the bite (al dente).
6. **Finish the risotto:**
   - Once the rice is cooked to your desired consistency, stir in the cooked mushrooms.

- Add the remaining tablespoon of butter, grated Parmesan cheese, and heavy cream. Stir until the butter and cheese are melted and the risotto is creamy.
7. **Season and serve:**
    - Season with salt and pepper to taste.
    - Garnish with chopped fresh parsley, if desired.
    - Serve the creamy mushroom risotto immediately while hot.

Tips:

- **Variations:** You can customize your mushroom risotto by adding other ingredients such as spinach, peas, or diced cooked chicken for additional flavor and texture.
- **Consistency:** Risotto should have a creamy texture, so adjust the amount of broth and cooking time accordingly to achieve this.
- **Storage:** Leftover risotto can be stored in an airtight container in the refrigerator for up to 3 days. Reheat gently on the stove with a splash of broth or cream to revive the creamy texture.

Creamy Mushroom Risotto is a delightful dish that showcases the earthy flavors of mushrooms and the creamy richness of Arborio rice. Enjoy making this comforting Italian favorite at home!

Bacon-Wrapped Jalapeno Poppers

Ingredients:

- 12 fresh jalapeno peppers
- 8 oz cream cheese, softened
- 1 cup shredded cheddar cheese
- 1 teaspoon garlic powder
- 1/2 teaspoon paprika
- Salt and pepper, to taste
- 12 slices bacon, cut in half crosswise
- Toothpicks or cocktail sticks

Instructions:

1. **Prepare the jalapenos:**
   - Preheat your oven to 400°F (200°C).
   - Cut each jalapeno pepper in half lengthwise. Remove the seeds and membranes to reduce the heat, or leave some in for spicier poppers.
2. **Make the filling:**
   - In a mixing bowl, combine the softened cream cheese, shredded cheddar cheese, garlic powder, paprika, salt, and pepper. Mix until well combined.
3. **Stuff the jalapenos:**
   - Spoon the cheese mixture into each jalapeno half, filling them evenly.
4. **Wrap with bacon:**
   - Wrap each stuffed jalapeno half with a half-slice of bacon, securing it with a toothpick or cocktail stick.
5. **Bake the poppers:**
   - Place the bacon-wrapped jalapeno poppers on a baking sheet lined with parchment paper or aluminum foil.
   - Bake in the preheated oven for 20-25 minutes, or until the bacon is crispy and the jalapenos are tender.
6. **Serve:**
   - Remove from the oven and let cool slightly before serving.
   - Serve warm as an appetizer or snack.

Tips:

- **Variations:** You can add finely chopped cooked chicken, shrimp, or even crab meat to the cream cheese mixture for added flavor and texture.
- **Grilling option:** These poppers can also be cooked on a grill over medium heat until the bacon is crispy and the jalapenos are tender.
- **Handling jalapenos:** Wear gloves when handling jalapeno peppers to protect your hands from the spicy oils. Avoid touching your face or eyes.

Bacon-wrapped jalapeno poppers are sure to be a hit at any gathering or party with their combination of creamy cheese, spicy jalapeno, and crispy bacon. Enjoy making and sharing these delicious treats!

Pork Belly Bites with BBQ Sauce

Ingredients:

- 1 lb pork belly, skin removed and cut into bite-sized pieces
- Salt and pepper, to taste
- 1 tablespoon olive oil
- 1/2 cup BBQ sauce (homemade or store-bought)
- Fresh parsley or cilantro, chopped (for garnish, optional)
- Toothpicks or cocktail sticks

Instructions:

1. **Preheat the oven:** Preheat your oven to 375°F (190°C).
2. **Prepare the pork belly:**
   - Pat dry the pork belly pieces with paper towels. Season generously with salt and pepper.
3. **Sear the pork belly:**
   - Heat olive oil in a large oven-safe skillet or cast-iron pan over medium-high heat.
   - Add the pork belly pieces in a single layer, ensuring they are not overcrowded. Sear each side until browned and crispy, about 2-3 minutes per side. This step helps render some of the fat and develop flavor.
4. **Add BBQ sauce:**
   - Remove the skillet from heat. Brush or spoon BBQ sauce over each pork belly bite, coating them evenly.
5. **Bake:**
   - Place the skillet in the preheated oven and bake for 15-20 minutes, or until the pork belly is cooked through and tender, and the BBQ sauce has caramelized slightly.
6. **Serve:**
   - Remove from the oven and let cool slightly.
   - Transfer the pork belly bites to a serving platter and garnish with chopped fresh parsley or cilantro, if desired.
   - Serve warm with additional BBQ sauce on the side for dipping, if desired.

Tips:

- **Crispy texture:** For extra crispy pork belly bites, you can broil them for the last few minutes of baking, watching closely to prevent burning.
- **Variations:** Experiment with different flavors of BBQ sauce, such as honey BBQ, smoky chipotle, or spicy Sriracha BBQ, to customize the taste according to your preference.
- **Make ahead:** You can prepare the pork belly bites ahead of time and reheat them in the oven before serving. This makes them perfect for parties or gatherings.

Pork belly bites with BBQ sauce are a delicious combination of tender pork belly and sweet, tangy BBQ flavors, making them a crowd-pleasing appetizer or snack. Enjoy making and sharing this tasty dish!

Beef Stroganoff with Sour Cream

Ingredients:

- 1 lb beef tenderloin or sirloin steak, thinly sliced into strips
- Salt and pepper, to taste
- 2 tablespoons olive oil or butter
- 1 onion, finely chopped
- 2 cloves garlic, minced
- 8 oz cremini mushrooms, sliced
- 1 tablespoon all-purpose flour
- 1 cup beef broth
- 1 tablespoon Dijon mustard
- 1 tablespoon Worcestershire sauce
- 1 cup sour cream
- 1 tablespoon fresh parsley, chopped (for garnish, optional)
- Cooked egg noodles, rice, or mashed potatoes (for serving)

Instructions:

1. **Prepare the beef:**
    - Season the beef strips with salt and pepper.
2. **Cook the beef:**
    - In a large skillet or frying pan, heat 1 tablespoon of olive oil or butter over medium-high heat.
    - Add the beef strips in batches and cook until browned on all sides, about 2-3 minutes per batch. Remove the beef from the skillet and set aside.
3. **Cook the vegetables:**
    - In the same skillet, add the remaining tablespoon of olive oil or butter if needed.
    - Add the chopped onion and cook until softened and translucent, about 3-4 minutes.
    - Add the minced garlic and sliced mushrooms. Cook until the mushrooms are browned and tender, about 5-6 minutes.
4. **Make the sauce:**
    - Sprinkle the flour over the mushrooms and onions. Stir well to combine and cook for 1-2 minutes to cook out the raw flour taste.
    - Gradually pour in the beef broth, stirring constantly to avoid lumps. Cook until the sauce thickens, about 3-4 minutes.
5. **Finish the dish:**
    - Stir in the Dijon mustard and Worcestershire sauce.
    - Return the cooked beef strips to the skillet.
    - Reduce the heat to low and stir in the sour cream. Cook gently for 2-3 minutes, stirring occasionally, until the beef is heated through and the sauce is creamy. Avoid boiling to prevent curdling of the sour cream.
    - Taste and adjust seasoning with salt and pepper if needed.

6. **Serve:**
    - Serve the Beef Stroganoff over cooked egg noodles, rice, or mashed potatoes.
    - Garnish with chopped fresh parsley, if desired.

Tips:

- **Cutting beef:** For easier slicing, place the beef in the freezer for about 20-30 minutes to firm it up before slicing into thin strips.
- **Variations:** You can substitute beef tenderloin or sirloin with other cuts of beef such as flank steak or chuck roast. Adjust cooking times accordingly for different cuts.
- **Storage:** Leftover Beef Stroganoff can be stored in an airtight container in the refrigerator for up to 3 days. Reheat gently on the stove with a splash of beef broth or water to maintain the creamy texture.

Beef Stroganoff with sour cream is a comforting and satisfying dish that's perfect for a cozy dinner. Enjoy making this classic recipe at home and savoring its creamy, flavorful sauce!

Salmon with Garlic Butter Sauce

Ingredients:

- 4 salmon fillets, skin-on or skinless (about 6 oz each)
- Salt and pepper, to taste
- 2 tablespoons olive oil
- 4 tablespoons unsalted butter
- 4 cloves garlic, minced
- 1/4 cup chicken or vegetable broth
- Juice of 1/2 lemon (about 1-2 tablespoons)
- 2 tablespoons chopped fresh parsley (optional, for garnish)
- Lemon wedges, for serving

Instructions:

1. **Season the salmon:**
   - Pat the salmon fillets dry with paper towels. Season both sides with salt and pepper.
2. **Cook the salmon:**
   - In a large skillet or frying pan, heat the olive oil over medium-high heat.
   - Place the salmon fillets in the skillet, skin-side down if using skin-on fillets. Cook for 3-4 minutes per side, depending on the thickness of the fillets, until golden brown and cooked to your desired doneness. Transfer the cooked salmon to a plate and cover to keep warm.
3. **Make the garlic butter sauce:**
   - In the same skillet, melt the butter over medium heat.
   - Add the minced garlic and cook for 1-2 minutes until fragrant, stirring constantly to prevent burning.
4. **Deglaze the skillet:**
   - Pour in the chicken or vegetable broth and lemon juice, stirring to combine. Bring to a simmer and cook for 2-3 minutes, allowing the sauce to reduce slightly.
5. **Finish the dish:**
   - Return the cooked salmon fillets to the skillet, spooning the garlic butter sauce over the top.
   - Cook for another 1-2 minutes, gently spooning the sauce over the salmon to coat.
6. **Serve:**
   - Remove from heat and garnish with chopped fresh parsley, if desired.
   - Serve the salmon with garlic butter sauce immediately, accompanied by lemon wedges for squeezing over the fish.

Tips:

- **Cooking time:** Adjust cooking time based on the thickness of your salmon fillets. The salmon is done when it flakes easily with a fork and reaches an internal temperature of 145°F (63°C).
- **Variations:** You can add capers, chopped sun-dried tomatoes, or a splash of white wine to the garlic butter sauce for additional flavor.
- **Side dishes:** Serve the salmon with garlic butter sauce alongside steamed vegetables, rice, quinoa, or a fresh green salad.

Salmon with garlic butter sauce is a simple yet elegant dish that's perfect for a weeknight dinner or a special occasion. Enjoy making and savoring this flavorful recipe!

Cheese Fondue with Bread and Vegetables

Ingredients:

- 1 garlic clove, halved
- 1 cup dry white wine (such as Sauvignon Blanc)
- 1 tablespoon lemon juice
- 8 oz Gruyere cheese, grated
- 8 oz Emmental cheese, grated
- 2 tablespoons all-purpose flour
- 1/2 teaspoon nutmeg, freshly grated
- Salt and pepper, to taste
- Assorted bread cubes (baguette, ciabatta, or any crusty bread)
- Assorted vegetables (such as broccoli florets, cauliflower florets, cherry tomatoes, baby potatoes, or bell pepper strips), blanched or steamed
- Optional: cured meats (such as cubed salami or prosciutto), apple slices, or pickles for dipping

Instructions:

1. **Prepare the fondue pot:**
   - Rub the inside of a fondue pot or a heavy-bottomed saucepan with the halved garlic clove.
   - Discard the garlic or leave it in the pot for extra flavor.
2. **Make the cheese mixture:**
   - In the fondue pot, combine the dry white wine and lemon juice. Heat over medium-low heat until it just starts to simmer (do not boil).
   - In a bowl, toss the grated Gruyere and Emmental cheeses with flour until well coated.
3. **Gradually add cheese to the pot:**
   - Gradually add handfuls of the cheese mixture to the simmering wine, stirring constantly in a figure-eight motion with a wooden spoon until the cheese is melted and smooth.
4. **Season and finish:**
   - Stir in the freshly grated nutmeg, and season with salt and pepper to taste.
5. **Serve:**
   - Place the fondue pot on a fondue burner or low heat source at the table.
   - Arrange the assorted bread cubes, blanched or steamed vegetables, and any optional dipping items on a platter around the fondue pot.
   - Spear the bread cubes, vegetables, and other items with fondue forks or skewers, and dip into the melted cheese.

Tips:

- **Maintaining consistency:** If the fondue becomes too thick, gradually stir in a little more white wine or lemon juice until it reaches your desired consistency.
- **Dipping:** Be creative with your dipping items! Besides bread and vegetables, you can also dip cooked meatballs, seafood, or even fruits like apple slices into the cheese fondue.
- **Leftovers:** Leftover fondue can be refrigerated and reheated gently on the stove with a splash of white wine or chicken broth to maintain its creamy texture.

Cheese fondue with bread and vegetables is a fun and interactive dish that brings people together. Enjoy the rich, cheesy goodness and experiment with different dipping combinations!

Hollandaise Sauce with Asparagus

Ingredients:

- 1 bunch of asparagus, woody ends trimmed
- Salt, to taste
- Lemon wedges (for serving)
- Freshly ground black pepper, to taste
- Optional: chopped fresh parsley or chives for garnish

For the Hollandaise Sauce:

- 3 large egg yolks
- 1 tablespoon lemon juice
- 1/2 cup (1 stick) unsalted butter, melted and hot
- Pinch of cayenne pepper (optional)
- Salt, to taste

Instructions:

1. **Prepare the asparagus:**
   - Bring a large pot of salted water to a boil.
   - Add the trimmed asparagus and cook until crisp-tender, about 3-4 minutes. Be careful not to overcook. Drain the asparagus and set aside.
2. **Make the Hollandaise sauce:**
   - Fill a saucepan with a couple of inches of water and bring it to a simmer over medium heat.
   - In a heatproof bowl that fits snugly over the saucepan (but does not touch the water), whisk together the egg yolks and lemon juice until smooth.
   - Place the bowl over the simmering water (creating a double boiler) and whisk continuously until the mixture thickens slightly and becomes pale yellow, about 2-3 minutes.
3. **Incorporate the butter:**
   - Slowly drizzle the hot melted butter into the egg yolk mixture, whisking constantly. Add the butter in a steady stream while whisking vigorously until all the butter is incorporated and the sauce is smooth and creamy.
4. **Season and serve:**
   - Remove the bowl from the heat and season the Hollandaise sauce with salt and cayenne pepper (if using).
   - Arrange the cooked asparagus on a serving platter or individual plates.
   - Spoon the Hollandaise sauce generously over the asparagus spears.
5. **Garnish and serve:**
   - Garnish with chopped fresh parsley or chives, if desired.
   - Serve immediately with lemon wedges on the side for extra flavor.

Tips:

- **Consistency:** If the Hollandaise sauce becomes too thick, you can thin it out with a little warm water or lemon juice, whisking continuously until you reach the desired consistency.
- **Timing:** Make sure the butter is hot when you add it to the egg yolk mixture to ensure proper emulsification and a smooth sauce.
- **Variations:** Hollandaise sauce pairs well with other vegetables such as steamed broccoli, green beans, or even over poached eggs for Eggs Benedict.

Hollandaise sauce with asparagus is a classic and elegant dish that's perfect for brunch, lunch, or a special dinner. Enjoy the creamy richness of the sauce alongside the freshness of the asparagus!

Chicken Alfredo Pizza with Extra Cheese

Ingredients:

- 1 pre-made pizza dough or store-bought pizza crust
- 1 cup Alfredo sauce (homemade or store-bought)
- 1 cup shredded cooked chicken breast
- 1 1/2 cups shredded mozzarella cheese
- 1/2 cup shredded Parmesan cheese
- 1/2 teaspoon garlic powder
- 1/2 teaspoon dried oregano
- Fresh parsley, chopped (for garnish, optional)

Instructions:

1. **Preheat the oven:**
   - Preheat your oven to the temperature recommended for your pizza crust (usually around 425°F or 220°C).
2. **Prepare the pizza crust:**
   - Roll out the pizza dough on a floured surface to your desired thickness. Place it on a pizza stone or baking sheet lined with parchment paper.
3. **Assemble the pizza:**
   - Spread the Alfredo sauce evenly over the pizza dough, leaving a small border around the edges for the crust.
   - Sprinkle the shredded mozzarella cheese over the Alfredo sauce.
   - Evenly distribute the shredded chicken over the cheese.
4. **Add extra cheese:**
   - Sprinkle the shredded Parmesan cheese over the top of the pizza.
   - Optionally, you can add extra mozzarella cheese or any other favorite cheese for even more cheesiness.
5. **Season:**
   - Sprinkle garlic powder and dried oregano over the top of the pizza for added flavor.
6. **Bake the pizza:**
   - Place the pizza in the preheated oven and bake according to the instructions for your pizza crust, usually about 12-15 minutes, or until the crust is golden brown and the cheese is melted and bubbly.
7. **Garnish and serve:**
   - Remove the pizza from the oven and let it cool slightly.
   - Garnish with chopped fresh parsley, if desired.
   - Slice the Chicken Alfredo pizza and serve hot.

Tips:

- **Chicken:** You can use leftover cooked chicken or rotisserie chicken for convenience. Season the chicken with salt, pepper, and any other favorite spices before shredding.
- **Variations:** Add your favorite toppings such as sliced mushrooms, spinach, or cherry tomatoes to customize the pizza to your liking.
- **Storage:** Leftover pizza can be stored in an airtight container in the refrigerator for up to 3 days. Reheat in the oven or toaster oven for best results.

Chicken Alfredo pizza with extra cheese is a delicious twist on classic pizza flavors, combining the creamy richness of Alfredo sauce with the savory goodness of chicken and cheese. Enjoy making and indulging in this flavorful pizza at home!

Creamy Shrimp Scampi Pasta

Ingredients:

- 8 oz (about 225g) linguine or fettuccine pasta
- 1 lb (about 450g) large shrimp, peeled and deveined
- Salt and pepper, to taste
- 2 tablespoons olive oil
- 4 tablespoons unsalted butter, divided
- 4 cloves garlic, minced
- 1/2 cup dry white wine (such as Sauvignon Blanc)
- 1 cup heavy cream
- Zest and juice of 1 lemon
- 1/2 teaspoon red pepper flakes (optional, adjust to taste)
- 1/2 cup grated Parmesan cheese
- 2 tablespoons chopped fresh parsley
- Lemon wedges, for serving
- Additional grated Parmesan cheese, for serving

Instructions:

1. **Cook the pasta:**
   - Cook the pasta in a large pot of salted boiling water according to package instructions until al dente. Drain and set aside.
2. **Prepare the shrimp:**
   - Season the shrimp with salt and pepper.
   - In a large skillet or frying pan, heat 1 tablespoon of olive oil over medium-high heat. Add the shrimp in a single layer and cook for 2-3 minutes per side until pink and cooked through. Remove the shrimp from the skillet and set aside.
3. **Make the creamy sauce:**
   - In the same skillet, melt 2 tablespoons of butter over medium heat. Add the minced garlic and cook for 1-2 minutes until fragrant.
   - Pour in the white wine and simmer for 2-3 minutes, scraping up any browned bits from the bottom of the skillet.
   - Stir in the heavy cream, lemon zest, lemon juice, and red pepper flakes (if using). Bring the mixture to a simmer.
4. **Combine pasta and sauce:**
   - Reduce the heat to low. Add the cooked pasta to the skillet and toss to coat in the creamy sauce.
   - Stir in the grated Parmesan cheese and remaining 2 tablespoons of butter until melted and smooth.
5. **Add shrimp and finish:**
   - Gently stir in the cooked shrimp and chopped parsley, reserving a little parsley for garnish.
   - Season with additional salt and pepper to taste, if needed.

6. **Serve:**
    - Divide the creamy shrimp scampi pasta among serving plates or bowls.
    - Garnish with chopped parsley and serve with lemon wedges and additional grated Parmesan cheese on the side.

Tips:

- **Pasta choice:** Linguine or fettuccine works well for this dish, but you can use any pasta shape you prefer.
- **Cream consistency:** If the sauce is too thick, you can thin it out with a little pasta cooking water or additional heavy cream.
- **Variations:** Add diced tomatoes, spinach, or capers to the sauce for additional flavor and color.

Creamy shrimp scampi pasta is a delightful and comforting dish that's perfect for a special dinner or a weekend indulgence. Enjoy making and savoring this flavorful pasta dish at home!

Loaded Cheese Fries with Bacon

Ingredients:

- 1 lb (about 450g) frozen French fries or homemade fries
- 8 slices bacon, cooked until crispy and chopped
- 1 1/2 cups shredded cheddar cheese (or your favorite cheese blend)
- 1/2 cup shredded mozzarella cheese (optional)
- 1/4 cup sliced green onions (scallions), for garnish
- Sour cream, for serving (optional)
- Salt and pepper, to taste

Instructions:

1. **Prepare the fries:**
    - Cook the French fries according to package instructions until golden and crispy. If using homemade fries, bake or fry them until crispy.
2. **Cook the bacon:**
    - While the fries are cooking, cook the bacon until crispy in a skillet or in the oven. Drain on paper towels and chop into small pieces.
3. **Assemble the loaded cheese fries:**
    - Preheat your oven to 400°F (200°C).
    - Arrange the cooked fries on a large baking sheet or oven-proof dish in a single layer.
    - Sprinkle the shredded cheddar cheese (and mozzarella cheese, if using) evenly over the fries.
4. **Add the toppings:**
    - Scatter the chopped crispy bacon over the cheese-topped fries.
5. **Bake the loaded fries:**
    - Place the loaded fries in the preheated oven and bake for about 5-7 minutes, or until the cheese is melted and bubbly.
6. **Finish and serve:**
    - Remove from the oven and sprinkle with sliced green onions.
    - Serve immediately with a dollop of sour cream on the side, if desired.
    - Season with salt and pepper to taste.

Tips:

- **Variations:** Customize your loaded cheese fries with additional toppings such as diced jalapenos, diced tomatoes, or a drizzle of ranch dressing.
- **Cheese options:** Experiment with different types of cheese such as pepper jack, Swiss, or Gouda for unique flavor combinations.
- **Baking tray:** Using a parchment-lined baking sheet helps prevent the fries from sticking and makes cleanup easier.

Loaded cheese fries with bacon are a crowd-pleasing appetizer or indulgent side dish that's perfect for parties, game day gatherings, or a fun family meal. Enjoy making and sharing these delicious loaded fries at home!

Cheesecake with Raspberry Sauce

Ingredients:

For the Cheesecake:

- 1 1/2 cups graham cracker crumbs
- 1/4 cup granulated sugar
- 1/2 cup unsalted butter, melted
- 24 oz (3 packages) cream cheese, softened
- 1 cup granulated sugar
- 3 large eggs
- 1 teaspoon vanilla extract
- 1/2 cup sour cream
- Fresh raspberries, for garnish (optional)

For the Raspberry Sauce:

- 12 oz fresh or frozen raspberries
- 1/4 cup granulated sugar
- 1 tablespoon lemon juice
- 1 teaspoon cornstarch (optional, for thickening)

Instructions:

1. **Prepare the crust:**
    - Preheat your oven to 325°F (160°C).
    - In a mixing bowl, combine the graham cracker crumbs, 1/4 cup sugar, and melted butter. Mix until the crumbs are evenly coated.
    - Press the mixture firmly into the bottom of a 9-inch springform pan, forming an even layer. Use the bottom of a measuring cup or glass to compact the crust.
2. **Bake the crust:**
    - Bake the crust in the preheated oven for 10 minutes. Remove from the oven and set aside to cool while you prepare the cheesecake filling.
3. **Make the cheesecake filling:**
    - In a large mixing bowl, beat the softened cream cheese until smooth and creamy.
    - Gradually add 1 cup of sugar and continue beating until well combined.
    - Add the eggs one at a time, mixing well after each addition.
    - Stir in the vanilla extract and sour cream until smooth and creamy.
4. **Bake the cheesecake:**
    - Pour the cheesecake filling over the cooled crust in the springform pan.
    - Smooth the top with a spatula.
    - Bake in the preheated oven for 50-60 minutes, or until the edges are set and the center is slightly jiggly.
5. **Cool and chill:**

- Remove the cheesecake from the oven and let it cool completely at room temperature.
- Once cooled, refrigerate the cheesecake for at least 4 hours or overnight to firm up.

6. **Make the raspberry sauce:**
    - In a saucepan, combine the raspberries, 1/4 cup sugar, and lemon juice.
    - Cook over medium heat, stirring occasionally, until the raspberries break down and release their juices, about 5-7 minutes.
    - Optional: If you prefer a thicker sauce, mix 1 teaspoon of cornstarch with 1 tablespoon of cold water until smooth. Stir the cornstarch mixture into the raspberry sauce and cook for an additional 1-2 minutes until thickened.
    - Remove from heat and let the sauce cool to room temperature.
7. **Serve:**
    - Remove the cheesecake from the springform pan and transfer it to a serving platter.
    - Drizzle the raspberry sauce over the top of the cheesecake just before serving.
    - Garnish with fresh raspberries, if desired.

Tips:

- **Storage:** Store any leftover cheesecake in the refrigerator, covered, for up to 5 days.
- **Variations:** You can use other berries such as strawberries or blueberries to make different fruit sauces.
- **Presentation:** For a decorative touch, you can use a toothpick or skewer to create swirls with the raspberry sauce on top of the cheesecake before chilling.

Cheesecake with raspberry sauce is a classic dessert that's perfect for special occasions or whenever you're craving something sweet and creamy. Enjoy making and savoring this delicious cheesecake with the vibrant flavors of raspberry sauce!

Buttered Lobster Tails

Ingredients:

- 4 lobster tails (about 4-6 oz each), thawed if frozen
- Salt and pepper, to taste
- 1/2 cup unsalted butter, melted
- 2 cloves garlic, minced (optional)
- Fresh lemon wedges, for serving
- Fresh parsley, chopped, for garnish (optional)

Instructions:

1. **Prepare the lobster tails:**
    - Use kitchen shears to carefully cut along the top of each lobster tail shell lengthwise, starting from the wider end to the tail.
    - Gently pull apart the shell to expose the lobster meat, keeping the shell intact. Remove any veins or debris.
2. **Season the lobster tails:**
    - Sprinkle the lobster meat with salt and pepper to taste.
3. **Prepare the butter mixture:**
    - In a small bowl, mix together the melted butter and minced garlic, if using.
4. **Baste and grill/bake the lobster tails:**
    - **Grilling Method:**
        - Preheat your grill to medium-high heat.
        - Place the lobster tails shell-side down on the grill grates.
        - Brush the exposed lobster meat generously with the butter mixture.
        - Grill for 5-7 minutes, basting occasionally with the butter mixture, until the lobster meat is opaque and cooked through. The internal temperature should reach 140°F (60°C).
    - **Oven Method:**
        - Preheat your oven to 425°F (220°C).
        - Place the lobster tails shell-side down on a baking sheet lined with parchment paper or foil.
        - Brush the exposed lobster meat generously with the butter mixture.
        - Bake for 10-12 minutes, basting halfway through with the butter mixture, until the lobster meat is opaque and cooked through.
5. **Serve:**
    - Transfer the cooked lobster tails to a serving platter.
    - Garnish with chopped fresh parsley, if desired.
    - Serve immediately with fresh lemon wedges on the side for squeezing over the lobster meat.

Tips:

- **Butter variations:** You can customize the butter mixture by adding herbs like thyme or tarragon, or a splash of white wine for extra flavor.
- **Grilling alternatives:** If you don't have a grill, you can broil the lobster tails in the oven for a similar effect. Place them on a broiler pan or baking sheet and broil for about 5-7 minutes, basting with butter as directed.
- **Presentation:** To serve, you can remove the lobster meat from the shell for easier eating or leave it in the shell for an elegant presentation.

Buttered lobster tails are a luxurious and elegant dish that's perfect for special occasions or a romantic dinner at home. Enjoy the tender, flavorful lobster meat paired with rich buttery goodness!

Creamy Tomato Basil Soup with Heavy Cream

Ingredients:

- 2 tablespoons olive oil
- 1 onion, diced
- 3 cloves garlic, minced
- 2 tablespoons tomato paste
- 2 (14 oz) cans diced tomatoes
- 1 (14 oz) can tomato sauce
- 2 cups vegetable or chicken broth
- 1 teaspoon sugar (optional, to balance acidity)
- Salt and pepper, to taste
- 1/2 cup heavy cream
- 1/4 cup fresh basil leaves, chopped (plus more for garnish)
- Grated Parmesan cheese, for serving (optional)
- Croutons or bread, for serving (optional)

Instructions:

1. **Sauté aromatics:**
   - Heat olive oil in a large pot or Dutch oven over medium heat. Add diced onion and sauté until softened and translucent, about 5-7 minutes.
   - Add minced garlic and tomato paste, and cook for another 1-2 minutes until fragrant.
2. **Simmer the soup:**
   - Stir in the diced tomatoes, tomato sauce, and broth. Bring to a simmer.
   - Add sugar (if using), salt, and pepper to taste. Reduce heat to low and let it simmer for 15-20 minutes, stirring occasionally.
3. **Blend the soup:**
   - Use an immersion blender directly in the pot to puree the soup until smooth. Alternatively, carefully transfer the soup in batches to a blender and blend until smooth.
4. **Add cream and basil:**
   - Stir in the heavy cream and chopped fresh basil. Simmer for an additional 5 minutes to heat through and allow the flavors to meld.
5. **Serve:**
   - Ladle the creamy tomato basil soup into bowls. Garnish with additional chopped basil leaves and grated Parmesan cheese, if desired.
   - Serve with croutons or crusty bread on the side for dipping.

Tips:

- **Consistency:** If you prefer a thicker soup, you can simmer it uncovered for longer to reduce the liquid. For a thinner soup, add a bit more broth or water.

- **Variations:** You can add a pinch of red pepper flakes for a hint of spice or a drizzle of balsamic glaze for added sweetness and depth of flavor.
- **Storage:** Store leftover soup in an airtight container in the refrigerator for up to 4-5 days. Reheat gently on the stove over low heat, stirring occasionally.

Creamy tomato basil soup with heavy cream is a comforting and satisfying meal on its own or paired with your favorite sandwiches or salads. Enjoy the rich tomato flavor complemented by the creamy texture and fragrant basil!

Avocado and Bacon Stuffed Mushrooms

Ingredients:

- 12 large white or cremini mushrooms, stems removed and cleaned
- 1 ripe avocado
- Juice of 1/2 lime
- Salt and pepper, to taste
- 4 slices bacon, cooked until crispy and crumbled
- 1/4 cup shredded mozzarella cheese (optional)
- 2 tablespoons chopped fresh cilantro or parsley, for garnish
- Lime wedges, for serving (optional)

Instructions:

1. **Prepare the mushrooms:**
   - Preheat your oven to 375°F (190°C).
   - Remove the stems from the mushrooms and gently scrape out the gills using a spoon. Place the mushrooms on a baking sheet lined with parchment paper or aluminum foil.
2. **Prepare the avocado mixture:**
   - In a bowl, mash the ripe avocado with a fork until smooth.
   - Stir in the lime juice and season with salt and pepper to taste.
3. **Combine avocado and bacon:**
   - Mix the crumbled bacon into the mashed avocado until well combined. Adjust seasoning if needed.
4. **Stuff the mushrooms:**
   - Spoon the avocado and bacon mixture into each mushroom cap, filling them generously. If using mozzarella cheese, sprinkle a little on top of each stuffed mushroom.
5. **Bake the stuffed mushrooms:**
   - Bake in the preheated oven for 12-15 minutes, or until the mushrooms are tender and the filling is heated through. If using cheese, it should be melted and bubbly.
6. **Garnish and serve:**
   - Remove the stuffed mushrooms from the oven and let them cool slightly.
   - Sprinkle chopped cilantro or parsley over the stuffed mushrooms for garnish.
   - Serve warm with lime wedges on the side for an extra burst of freshness.

Tips:

- **Variations:** You can add a dash of hot sauce or sprinkle with red pepper flakes for a spicy kick. Alternatively, top with a dollop of sour cream or Greek yogurt.
- **Make-ahead:** You can prepare the avocado and bacon mixture ahead of time and store it in the refrigerator. When ready to serve, simply stuff the mushrooms and bake.

- **Presentation:** For a fancier presentation, sprinkle some extra chopped herbs or a drizzle of balsamic reduction over the stuffed mushrooms before serving.

Avocado and bacon stuffed mushrooms are a flavorful and satisfying appetizer that's sure to impress your guests or family. Enjoy the creamy avocado, crispy bacon, and earthy mushrooms in every bite!

Chocolate Peanut Butter Fat Bombs

Ingredients:

- 1/2 cup natural peanut butter (unsweetened)
- 1/4 cup coconut oil, melted
- 2 tablespoons cocoa powder (unsweetened)
- 2-3 tablespoons powdered erythritol or sweetener of choice, to taste
- 1/2 teaspoon vanilla extract
- Pinch of salt

Instructions:

1. **Prepare the mixture:**
   - In a mixing bowl, combine the melted coconut oil, natural peanut butter, cocoa powder, powdered sweetener, vanilla extract, and a pinch of salt. Mix well until smooth and well combined.
2. **Shape the fat bombs:**
   - Line a mini muffin tin with paper liners or use silicone molds.
   - Spoon the chocolate peanut butter mixture evenly into each mold, filling them almost to the top.
3. **Chill:**
   - Place the muffin tin or molds in the refrigerator or freezer to set for at least 1 hour, or until firm.
4. **Serve:**
   - Once set, remove the fat bombs from the molds.
   - Store them in an airtight container in the refrigerator until ready to serve.

Tips:

- **Variations:** You can customize these fat bombs by adding chopped nuts (like almonds or walnuts), shredded coconut, or a sprinkle of sea salt on top for extra flavor and texture.
- **Sweetener:** Adjust the sweetness level to your preference by adding more or less powdered sweetener.
- **Storage:** Store the fat bombs in the refrigerator for up to 1-2 weeks, or in the freezer for longer storage. Let them sit at room temperature for a few minutes before enjoying if stored in the freezer.

These chocolate peanut butter fat bombs are a perfect guilt-free treat to satisfy your sweet cravings while providing a boost of healthy fats. Enjoy them as a snack or dessert on a ketogenic or low-carb diet!

Creamy Spinach Artichoke Dip

Ingredients:

- 1 tablespoon olive oil
- 1 small onion, finely chopped
- 2 cloves garlic, minced
- 1 (8 oz) package cream cheese, softened
- 1/2 cup sour cream
- 1/2 cup mayonnaise
- 1/2 cup grated Parmesan cheese
- 1/2 cup shredded mozzarella cheese
- 1 (14 oz) can artichoke hearts, drained and chopped
- 1 (10 oz) package frozen chopped spinach, thawed and excess water squeezed out
- 1/2 teaspoon salt, or to taste
- 1/4 teaspoon black pepper
- 1/4 teaspoon red pepper flakes (optional, for a bit of heat)
- Tortilla chips, bread, or crackers, for serving

Instructions:

1. **Prepare the spinach and artichokes:**
   - Thaw the frozen spinach and squeeze out excess water using a clean kitchen towel or paper towels. Chop the artichoke hearts into smaller pieces if they are not already chopped.
2. **Sauté onions and garlic:**
   - In a skillet, heat olive oil over medium heat. Add chopped onion and cook until softened, about 3-4 minutes. Add minced garlic and cook for another 1-2 minutes until fragrant. Remove from heat and set aside.
3. **Mix the dip ingredients:**
   - In a mixing bowl, combine softened cream cheese, sour cream, mayonnaise, grated Parmesan cheese, shredded mozzarella cheese, sautéed onions and garlic, chopped artichoke hearts, chopped spinach, salt, black pepper, and red pepper flakes (if using). Mix until well combined.
4. **Bake the dip:**
   - Preheat your oven to 350°F (175°C).
   - Transfer the spinach artichoke mixture to a baking dish (about 8x8 inches or similar size) and spread it evenly.
5. **Bake the dip:**
   - Bake in the preheated oven for 25-30 minutes, or until the dip is bubbly and lightly golden on top.
6. **Serve:**
   - Remove from the oven and let the dip cool slightly before serving.
   - Serve warm with tortilla chips, bread, or crackers for dipping.

Tips:

- **Make-ahead:** You can prepare the spinach artichoke dip ahead of time and refrigerate it before baking. When ready to serve, bake as directed.
- **Variations:** Add a sprinkle of additional cheese on top before baking for extra cheesiness. You can also add diced cooked bacon or chopped roasted red peppers for additional flavor.
- **Storage:** Store any leftover dip in an airtight container in the refrigerator for up to 3-4 days. Reheat gently in the oven or microwave before serving.

Creamy spinach artichoke dip is sure to be a crowd-pleaser at any gathering. Enjoy the creamy texture and delicious flavors of this classic appetizer!

Coconut Milk Curry with Chicken

Ingredients:

- 1 lb (450g) chicken breast or thighs, cut into bite-sized pieces
- 2 tablespoons vegetable oil
- 1 onion, finely chopped
- 3 cloves garlic, minced
- 1 tablespoon fresh ginger, grated or minced
- 1 tablespoon curry powder
- 1 teaspoon ground cumin
- 1 teaspoon ground coriander
- 1/2 teaspoon turmeric powder
- 1/4 teaspoon cayenne pepper (adjust to taste)
- 1 can (14 oz / 400ml) coconut milk
- 1 cup chicken broth
- 1 tablespoon soy sauce or fish sauce
- 1 tablespoon brown sugar or coconut sugar (optional, for sweetness)
- Salt and pepper, to taste
- Fresh cilantro, chopped, for garnish
- Cooked rice or naan, for serving

Instructions:

1. **Sauté the chicken:** Heat vegetable oil in a large skillet or pot over medium-high heat. Add the chicken pieces and cook until browned on all sides, about 5-7 minutes. Remove the chicken from the skillet and set aside.
2. **Sauté aromatics:** In the same skillet, add a bit more oil if needed. Add chopped onion and sauté until softened, about 3-4 minutes. Add minced garlic and grated ginger, and cook for another 1-2 minutes until fragrant.
3. **Add spices:** Stir in curry powder, ground cumin, ground coriander, turmeric powder, and cayenne pepper. Cook the spices for about 1 minute until aromatic.
4. **Simmer with coconut milk and broth:** Pour in the coconut milk and chicken broth, stirring to combine. Bring the mixture to a simmer.
5. **Combine and simmer:** Return the browned chicken to the skillet. Add soy sauce or fish sauce and brown sugar (if using). Season with salt and pepper to taste. Stir well to combine.
6. **Simmer and thicken:** Reduce the heat to medium-low and let the curry simmer uncovered for 15-20 minutes, stirring occasionally, until the chicken is cooked through and the sauce has thickened.
7. **Serve:** Remove from heat and garnish with chopped fresh cilantro. Serve hot over cooked rice or with naan bread.

Tips:

- **Vegetables:** You can add vegetables such as bell peppers, carrots, or peas to the curry for added texture and flavor. Add them along with the chicken broth to cook until tender.
- **Spice level:** Adjust the amount of cayenne pepper or omit it entirely based on your spice preference. You can also add more curry powder for a stronger curry flavor.
- **Make-ahead:** This curry tastes even better the next day as the flavors meld together. Store leftovers in an airtight container in the refrigerator for up to 3 days.

Coconut milk curry with chicken is a comforting and aromatic dish that's perfect for a weeknight dinner. Enjoy the creamy coconut sauce infused with spices and tender chicken!

Mascarpone-Stuffed Strawberries

Ingredients:

- 1 pound (about 16-20) large strawberries
- 8 oz mascarpone cheese, softened
- 1/4 cup powdered sugar (adjust to taste)
- 1 teaspoon vanilla extract
- Zest of 1 lemon (optional, for extra flavor)
- Fresh mint leaves, for garnish (optional)

Instructions:

1. **Prepare the strawberries:**
   - Rinse the strawberries under cold water and pat them dry with paper towels.
   - Cut off the tops of the strawberries and use a small paring knife to carefully hollow out the center of each strawberry to create a cavity. Be careful not to cut all the way through.
2. **Make the mascarpone filling:**
   - In a mixing bowl, combine the softened mascarpone cheese, powdered sugar, vanilla extract, and lemon zest (if using). Mix until smooth and well combined. Taste and adjust sweetness if needed.
3. **Fill the strawberries:**
   - Transfer the mascarpone filling into a piping bag fitted with a star or round tip, or simply use a small spoon.
   - Carefully pipe or spoon the mascarpone mixture into each hollowed-out strawberry, filling them just to the top.
4. **Chill and garnish:**
   - Arrange the stuffed strawberries on a serving platter.
   - Optional: Garnish each strawberry with a small mint leaf for decoration.
5. **Serve:**
   - Serve the mascarpone-stuffed strawberries immediately, or refrigerate them for 30 minutes to 1 hour to chill before serving.

Tips:

- **Variations:** You can add a drizzle of melted chocolate over the stuffed strawberries for an extra touch of indulgence. Alternatively, sprinkle chopped nuts such as pistachios or almonds on top for added crunch.
- **Presentation:** For a beautiful presentation, arrange the stuffed strawberries on a bed of powdered sugar or cocoa powder. You can also serve them in individual dessert cups or on decorative serving trays.
- **Make-ahead:** You can prepare the mascarpone filling and hollow out the strawberries ahead of time. Store the filling and strawberries separately in the refrigerator. Fill the strawberries with the mascarpone mixture just before serving to keep them fresh.

Mascarpone-stuffed strawberries are a perfect dessert for parties, gatherings, or simply as a sweet treat. Enjoy the creamy mascarpone filling paired with juicy strawberries for a delicious bite-sized dessert!

Garlic Parmesan Wings

Ingredients:

- 2 lbs chicken wings, split into drumettes and flats
- Salt and pepper, to taste
- 1/2 cup unsalted butter
- 4 cloves garlic, minced
- 1/2 cup grated Parmesan cheese
- 1 tablespoon chopped fresh parsley (optional, for garnish)
- Lemon wedges, for serving (optional)

Instructions:

1. **Preheat the oven:**
   - Preheat your oven to 400°F (200°C). Line a baking sheet with aluminum foil and place a wire rack on top.
2. **Prepare the chicken wings:**
   - Pat dry the chicken wings with paper towels to remove excess moisture. Season generously with salt and pepper.
3. **Bake the chicken wings:**
   - Arrange the seasoned chicken wings in a single layer on the wire rack. Bake in the preheated oven for 40-45 minutes, flipping halfway through, until the wings are crispy and cooked through.
4. **Make the garlic Parmesan sauce:**
   - In a small saucepan, melt the butter over medium heat. Add the minced garlic and sauté for 1-2 minutes until fragrant, being careful not to burn the garlic.
5. **Coat the wings:**
   - Remove the baked wings from the oven and transfer them to a large mixing bowl.
   - Pour the melted garlic butter over the wings and toss them until evenly coated.
6. **Add Parmesan cheese:**
   - Sprinkle grated Parmesan cheese over the wings and toss again to coat them evenly with the cheese.
7. **Serve:**
   - Transfer the garlic Parmesan wings to a serving platter. Garnish with chopped fresh parsley, if desired.
   - Serve hot with lemon wedges on the side for squeezing over the wings, if desired.

Tips:

- **Variations:** For extra flavor, you can add a pinch of red pepper flakes or dried herbs (such as oregano or thyme) to the garlic butter sauce.

- **Grilled option:** Instead of baking, you can grill the seasoned chicken wings over medium-high heat for about 20-25 minutes, turning occasionally, until they are cooked through and crispy.
- **Storage:** Garlic Parmesan wings are best enjoyed fresh and hot. If you have leftovers, store them in an airtight container in the refrigerator for up to 2 days. Reheat in the oven to maintain crispiness.

Garlic Parmesan wings are a crowd-pleasing appetizer or main dish that's perfect for game days, parties, or any occasion. Enjoy the savory garlic butter and Parmesan cheese coating combined with tender, crispy chicken wings!

Creamy Parmesan Polenta

Ingredients:

- 1 cup polenta (cornmeal)
- 4 cups water or chicken broth (or a combination of both)
- 1 teaspoon salt, or to taste
- 1/2 cup grated Parmesan cheese
- 2 tablespoons unsalted butter
- Freshly ground black pepper, to taste
- Chopped fresh parsley or basil, for garnish (optional)

Instructions:

1. **Cook the polenta:**
   - In a large saucepan, bring the water or chicken broth to a boil over medium-high heat. Gradually whisk in the polenta, stirring constantly to prevent lumps.
2. **Simmer:**
   - Reduce the heat to low and simmer the polenta, stirring frequently with a wooden spoon or silicone spatula, until it thickens and the grains are tender, about 20-30 minutes. Be careful as the polenta can bubble and splatter.
3. **Add Parmesan and butter:**
   - Once the polenta reaches a creamy consistency, stir in the grated Parmesan cheese and unsalted butter. Continue to stir until the cheese is melted and the butter is fully incorporated.
4. **Season and serve:**
   - Taste the polenta and season with salt and freshly ground black pepper, adjusting to your preference.
   - Remove the polenta from heat and transfer it to a serving bowl or dish.
5. **Garnish and serve:**
   - Garnish the creamy Parmesan polenta with chopped fresh parsley or basil, if desired.
   - Serve immediately while warm as a side dish with grilled meats, roasted vegetables, or as a base for braised meats and stews.

Tips:

- **Consistency:** If the polenta becomes too thick, you can thin it out with a little more water, broth, or milk until you reach your desired consistency.
- **Variations:** Add extra flavor by stirring in minced garlic, chopped fresh herbs (such as thyme or rosemary), or a splash of heavy cream or milk for extra creaminess.
- **Leftovers:** Leftover polenta can be stored in an airtight container in the refrigerator for up to 3 days. Reheat gently on the stovetop or in the microwave, adding a splash of water or broth to loosen it up.

Creamy Parmesan polenta is a comforting dish that pairs well with a variety of main courses and adds a touch of elegance to any meal. Enjoy its creamy texture and rich Parmesan flavor!

Pecan Pie with Whipped Cream

Ingredients:

For the pie crust:

- 1 1/4 cups all-purpose flour
- 1/2 teaspoon salt
- 1/2 teaspoon granulated sugar
- 1/2 cup unsalted butter, cold and cut into cubes
- 2-4 tablespoons ice water

For the pecan pie filling:

- 1 cup granulated sugar
- 1 cup light corn syrup
- 1/2 cup unsalted butter, melted and cooled slightly
- 1 teaspoon vanilla extract
- 1/4 teaspoon salt
- 3 large eggs, lightly beaten
- 1 1/2 cups pecan halves or chopped pecans

For the whipped cream:

- 1 cup heavy cream, chilled
- 2 tablespoons powdered sugar (or to taste)
- 1 teaspoon vanilla extract

Instructions:

1. **Prepare the pie crust:**
   - In a large mixing bowl, combine the flour, salt, and granulated sugar. Add the cold cubed butter.
   - Use a pastry cutter or fork to cut the butter into the flour mixture until it resembles coarse crumbs.
   - Gradually add ice water, 1 tablespoon at a time, mixing gently with a fork until the dough starts to come together.
   - Gather the dough into a ball, flatten it into a disc, wrap it in plastic wrap, and refrigerate for at least 30 minutes.
2. **Preheat the oven:**
   - Preheat your oven to 350°F (175°C).
3. **Roll out the pie crust:**
   - On a lightly floured surface, roll out the chilled dough into a circle large enough to fit into a 9-inch pie dish. Transfer the dough to the pie dish, gently press it into the bottom and sides, and trim any excess dough. Crimp the edges as desired.
4. **Prepare the pecan pie filling:**

- In a large mixing bowl, whisk together granulated sugar, corn syrup, melted butter, vanilla extract, and salt until well combined.
- Add the lightly beaten eggs and stir until smooth.
- Fold in the pecan halves or chopped pecans.

5. **Assemble and bake the pie:**
    - Pour the pecan pie filling into the prepared pie crust.
    - Place the pie on a baking sheet to catch any drips and bake in the preheated oven for 50-60 minutes, or until the filling is set and slightly puffed. The center should jiggle slightly when gently shaken.
6. **Cool the pie:**
    - Remove the pecan pie from the oven and allow it to cool completely on a wire rack before slicing.
7. **Make the whipped cream:**
    - In a chilled mixing bowl, beat the heavy cream, powdered sugar, and vanilla extract with an electric mixer on medium-high speed until soft peaks form.
8. **Serve:**
    - Slice the cooled pecan pie and serve each slice with a dollop of whipped cream on top.
    - Optionally, garnish with additional pecan halves or a sprinkle of powdered sugar before serving.

Tips:

- **Make-ahead:** You can prepare the pie crust and pecan pie filling ahead of time. Store the pie crust wrapped in plastic wrap in the refrigerator for up to 2 days. Store the pecan pie filling covered in the refrigerator for up to 1 day before baking.
- **Storage:** Leftover pecan pie can be stored covered at room temperature for up to 2 days or in the refrigerator for up to 4-5 days. The whipped cream should be stored separately and added fresh when serving.

Pecan pie with whipped cream is a decadent dessert that's perfect for holidays and special occasions. Enjoy the rich flavors of the pecan filling paired with the lightness of freshly whipped cream!

Blue Cheese and Bacon Burger

Ingredients:

- 1 lb ground beef (preferably 80/20 blend)
- Salt and pepper, to taste
- 4 hamburger buns, split and toasted
- 4 slices bacon, cooked until crispy
- 4 oz blue cheese, crumbled
- Lettuce leaves, tomato slices, red onion slices (optional, for topping)
- Condiments of choice (ketchup, mustard, mayonnaise)

Instructions:

1. **Prepare the bacon:**
    - Cook the bacon in a skillet over medium heat until crispy. Remove from the skillet and drain on paper towels. Set aside.
2. **Form the burger patties:**
    - Divide the ground beef into 4 equal portions. Shape each portion into a patty that matches the size of your hamburger buns. Press a slight indentation into the center of each patty to prevent it from puffing up while cooking. Season both sides of each patty with salt and pepper.
3. **Cook the burger patties:**
    - Heat a grill pan or skillet over medium-high heat. Cook the burger patties for about 4-5 minutes per side, or until they reach your desired level of doneness (medium-rare to well-done). During the last minute of cooking, top each patty with crumbled blue cheese and cover the pan briefly to allow the cheese to melt.
4. **Assemble the burgers:**
    - Place the toasted hamburger buns on a serving plate. Spread condiments of your choice on the bottom bun (such as ketchup, mustard, or mayonnaise).
    - Place a lettuce leaf on the bottom bun, followed by the cooked burger patty with melted blue cheese.
    - Top each burger patty with a slice of crispy bacon.
    - Add tomato slices and red onion slices (if using).
    - Close the burgers with the top bun and secure with a toothpick if necessary.
5. **Serve:**
    - Serve the Blue Cheese and Bacon Burgers immediately while hot. Optionally, serve with a side of fries, coleslaw, or a salad.

Tips:

- **Cheese variation:** If you prefer a milder cheese flavor, you can substitute blue cheese with another type of cheese such as cheddar, Swiss, or gouda.
- **Bacon preparation:** For a crispier texture, bake the bacon in the oven at 400°F (200°C) for about 15-20 minutes until crispy.

- **Customize toppings:** Feel free to customize the toppings based on your preference. You can add avocado slices, caramelized onions, or a drizzle of barbecue sauce for extra flavor.

Enjoy these juicy Blue Cheese and Bacon Burgers with your favorite toppings for a satisfying and flavorful meal that's perfect for any burger lover!

Loaded Nachos with Guacamole and Sour Cream

Ingredients:

- 1 bag (10-12 oz) tortilla chips
- 1 cup shredded cheddar cheese
- 1 cup shredded Monterey Jack cheese
- 1 cup black beans, drained and rinsed
- 1 cup corn kernels (fresh, canned, or frozen)
- 1/2 cup diced tomatoes
- 1/2 cup sliced black olives
- 1/4 cup sliced jalapeños (optional, for heat)
- 1/4 cup chopped fresh cilantro
- 1/4 cup diced red onion
- Guacamole (store-bought or homemade)
- Sour cream
- Salsa (optional, for serving)

Instructions:

1. **Preheat the oven:**
   - Preheat your oven to 375°F (190°C). Line a large baking sheet with parchment paper or aluminum foil for easy cleanup.
2. **Arrange the tortilla chips:**
   - Spread a single layer of tortilla chips evenly on the prepared baking sheet.
3. **Add cheese and toppings:**
   - Sprinkle shredded cheddar cheese and shredded Monterey Jack cheese evenly over the tortilla chips.
   - Scatter black beans, corn kernels, diced tomatoes, sliced black olives, and sliced jalapeños (if using) over the cheese.
4. **Bake the nachos:**
   - Place the loaded nachos in the preheated oven and bake for 10-12 minutes, or until the cheese is melted and bubbly.
5. **Garnish and serve:**
   - Remove the nachos from the oven and immediately drizzle with guacamole and sour cream.
   - Sprinkle chopped fresh cilantro and diced red onion over the top.
   - Serve the loaded nachos hot, optionally with salsa on the side.

Tips:

- **Variations:** Customize the loaded nachos with your favorite toppings such as cooked ground beef or shredded chicken, diced avocado, green onions, or pico de gallo.
- **Homemade guacamole:** To make quick guacamole, mash ripe avocados with lime juice, salt, and diced tomatoes. Adjust seasoning to taste.

- **Presentation:** Serve loaded nachos directly on the baking sheet for a casual gathering or transfer them to a large platter for a party.
- **Make-ahead:** Prepare the toppings and assemble the nachos just before baking to keep the chips crispy. Leftover toppings can be stored separately and used for another batch.

Loaded nachos with guacamole and sour cream are perfect for game day snacks, parties, or a fun family dinner. Enjoy the combination of crunchy chips, gooey cheese, and flavorful toppings!

Bacon-Wrapped Scallops

Ingredients:

- 12 large sea scallops, patted dry with paper towels
- 6 slices bacon, cut in half crosswise
- 1 tablespoon olive oil
- Freshly ground black pepper, to taste
- Toothpicks or small skewers

For the marinade (optional):

- 2 tablespoons soy sauce
- 1 tablespoon honey or maple syrup
- 1 clove garlic, minced
- 1 teaspoon grated fresh ginger

Instructions:

1. **Prepare the scallops:**
    - If using, combine the soy sauce, honey or maple syrup, minced garlic, and grated ginger in a bowl to make the marinade. Add the scallops to the marinade and toss gently to coat. Let marinate for 15-30 minutes while you prepare the bacon.
2. **Preheat the oven:**
    - Preheat your oven to 400°F (200°C). Line a baking sheet with aluminum foil and place a wire rack on top.
3. **Wrap the scallops with bacon:**
    - Wrap each scallop with a half-slice of bacon and secure it with a toothpick or small skewer. Repeat for all scallops.
4. **Cook the scallops:**
    - Heat olive oil in a large skillet over medium-high heat. Place the bacon-wrapped scallops in the skillet and cook for 2-3 minutes on each side, or until the bacon is slightly crispy. You may need to cook them in batches to avoid overcrowding the skillet.
5. **Transfer to the oven:**
    - Transfer the seared bacon-wrapped scallops to the prepared baking sheet with the wire rack. Season with freshly ground black pepper.
6. **Bake:**
    - Bake the scallops in the preheated oven for 10-12 minutes, or until the scallops are opaque and cooked through, and the bacon is crispy.
7. **Serve:**
    - Remove the bacon-wrapped scallops from the oven and let them rest for a few minutes. Remove the toothpicks or skewers before serving.
    - Serve the bacon-wrapped scallops hot as an appetizer with a squeeze of lemon juice, or as a main dish with sides like rice, vegetables, or a salad.

Tips:

- **Quality of ingredients:** Use large, dry-packed sea scallops for the best texture and flavor. Pat them dry with paper towels before wrapping with bacon to ensure crispiness.
- **Variations:** Instead of baking, you can also grill the bacon-wrapped scallops over medium-high heat on a preheated grill, turning occasionally, until the bacon is crispy and the scallops are cooked through.
- **Presentation:** Garnish with chopped fresh herbs like parsley or chives before serving for added color and flavor.

Bacon-wrapped scallops are a delightful dish that combines the richness of bacon with the delicate sweetness of scallops, making it a perfect appetizer or main course for special occasions or gatherings. Enjoy the savory flavors and crispy texture of this tasty dish!

Creamy Carbonara Pasta

Ingredients:

- 12 oz (340g) spaghetti or fettuccine
- 4 large eggs
- 1 cup grated Parmesan cheese, plus extra for serving
- 8 oz (225g) pancetta or bacon, diced
- 4 cloves garlic, minced
- 1/2 cup heavy cream (optional, for extra creaminess)
- Salt and freshly ground black pepper, to taste
- Fresh parsley, chopped (optional, for garnish)

Instructions:

1. **Cook the pasta:**
   - Bring a large pot of salted water to a boil. Add the pasta and cook according to package instructions until al dente. Reserve about 1 cup of pasta cooking water, then drain the pasta.
2. **Prepare the sauce:**
   - In a bowl, whisk together the eggs and grated Parmesan cheese until well combined. Set aside.
3. **Cook the pancetta (or bacon):**
   - In a large skillet or frying pan, cook the diced pancetta or bacon over medium heat until crispy and browned. Remove the pancetta from the pan and drain on paper towels, leaving the rendered fat in the pan.
4. **Make the Carbonara sauce:**
   - Add the minced garlic to the skillet with the pancetta fat and cook over medium heat for about 1 minute, until fragrant.
   - Reduce the heat to low. Slowly pour the egg and Parmesan mixture into the skillet, stirring quickly to coat the pasta. The residual heat will cook the eggs and create a creamy sauce. If using, stir in the heavy cream at this stage for extra creaminess.
5. **Combine the pasta and sauce:**
   - Add the cooked pasta to the skillet with the sauce, tossing gently to coat the pasta evenly. If the sauce seems too thick, gradually add some of the reserved pasta cooking water until desired consistency is reached.
6. **Add pancetta and season:**
   - Stir in the cooked pancetta or bacon. Season with salt and freshly ground black pepper to taste. Be cautious with salt as the pancetta or bacon and Parmesan are already salty.
7. **Serve:**
   - Divide the Creamy Carbonara Pasta among serving plates or bowls. Sprinkle with additional grated Parmesan cheese and chopped fresh parsley for garnish, if desired.

- Serve immediately while hot.

Tips:

- **Egg tempering:** To prevent the eggs from scrambling when adding them to the hot pasta, it's important to temper them slowly with the pasta cooking water or the heat from the skillet.
- **Variations:** You can add other ingredients such as peas, mushrooms, or cooked chicken to customize your Carbonara pasta.
- **Storage:** Creamy Carbonara pasta is best served fresh and hot. Leftovers can be stored in an airtight container in the refrigerator for up to 2 days. Reheat gently on the stove with a splash of milk or cream to revive the creaminess.

Enjoy this Creamy Carbonara Pasta recipe as a comforting and satisfying meal that's perfect for any occasion!

Keto Fathead Pizza with Pepperoni and Cheese

Ingredients:

For the Fathead pizza crust:

- 1 1/2 cups shredded mozzarella cheese
- 2 tablespoons cream cheese
- 1 cup almond flour
- 1 large egg
- 1/2 teaspoon salt
- 1/2 teaspoon garlic powder
- 1/2 teaspoon dried Italian seasoning (optional)

For the pizza toppings:

- 1/2 cup low-carb marinara sauce or pizza sauce
- 1 cup shredded mozzarella cheese
- 1/2 cup sliced pepperoni
- Fresh basil leaves, chopped (optional, for garnish)

Instructions:

1. **Preheat the oven:**
   - Preheat your oven to 425°F (220°C). Line a baking sheet or pizza stone with parchment paper.
2. **Make the Fathead pizza crust:**
   - In a microwave-safe bowl, combine the shredded mozzarella cheese and cream cheese. Microwave in 30-second intervals, stirring in between, until the cheese is melted and smooth.
3. **Mix the dough:**
   - To the melted cheese mixture, add almond flour, egg, salt, garlic powder, and dried Italian seasoning (if using). Mix until a dough forms. If the dough becomes too stiff to work with, you can microwave it for another 10-15 seconds to soften it.
4. **Form the pizza crust:**
   - Place the dough on the prepared baking sheet lined with parchment paper. Place another piece of parchment paper on top of the dough and use your hands or a rolling pin to flatten and shape the dough into a circle or rectangle, about 1/4 inch thick.
5. **Par-bake the crust:**
   - Bake the crust in the preheated oven for 8-10 minutes, until it is set and just starting to turn golden brown around the edges.
6. **Add the toppings:**
   - Remove the par-baked crust from the oven and spread low-carb marinara sauce or pizza sauce evenly over the crust.

- Sprinkle shredded mozzarella cheese over the sauce, then arrange sliced pepperoni on top.

7. **Bake the pizza:**
   - Return the pizza to the oven and bake for an additional 8-10 minutes, or until the cheese is melted and bubbly, and the crust is golden brown.
8. **Serve:**
   - Remove the Keto Fathead Pizza from the oven and let it cool slightly. Garnish with chopped fresh basil leaves, if desired.
   - Slice and serve hot.

Tips:

- **Variations:** Customize your Fathead Pizza with your favorite low-carb toppings such as cooked sausage, bell peppers, mushrooms, or olives.
- **Storage:** Leftover Keto Fathead Pizza can be stored in an airtight container in the refrigerator for up to 3 days. Reheat in the oven or toaster oven to maintain crispiness.
- **Almond flour substitution:** If you prefer, you can use coconut flour instead of almond flour, but you may need to adjust the quantity as coconut flour absorbs more moisture.

This Keto Fathead Pizza with pepperoni and cheese is a satisfying and flavorful option for those following a low-carb or ketogenic diet. Enjoy the cheesy goodness without the guilt of traditional pizza crust!

Cheesy Garlic Bread

Ingredients:

- 1 loaf of French bread or Italian bread
- 1/2 cup unsalted butter, softened
- 4 cloves garlic, minced
- 1/4 cup fresh parsley, finely chopped (optional)
- 1 1/2 cups shredded mozzarella cheese
- 1/2 cup grated Parmesan cheese
- Salt and pepper, to taste

Instructions:

1. **Preheat the oven:**
   - Preheat your oven to 375°F (190°C). Line a baking sheet with parchment paper or aluminum foil for easy cleanup.
2. **Prepare the garlic butter:**
   - In a small bowl, mix together the softened butter, minced garlic, and chopped parsley (if using). Season with salt and pepper to taste.
3. **Prepare the bread:**
   - Slice the loaf of French or Italian bread in half horizontally, creating two long halves.
4. **Spread the garlic butter:**
   - Spread the garlic butter evenly over the cut sides of the bread halves. Make sure to cover the entire surface area.
5. **Add the cheese:**
   - Sprinkle shredded mozzarella cheese evenly over the garlic buttered bread halves.
   - Sprinkle grated Parmesan cheese on top of the mozzarella cheese.
6. **Bake the garlic bread:**
   - Place the prepared garlic bread on the lined baking sheet.
   - Bake in the preheated oven for 12-15 minutes, or until the cheese is melted and bubbly, and the edges of the bread are golden brown.
7. **Serve:**
   - Remove the cheesy garlic bread from the oven and let it cool slightly.
   - Cut into slices and serve warm.

Tips:

- **Variations:** You can customize your cheesy garlic bread by adding other cheeses such as cheddar, provolone, or Gouda. You can also sprinkle some red pepper flakes for a bit of heat.
- **Herb options:** Instead of or in addition to parsley, you can use fresh herbs like basil, thyme, or oregano to enhance the flavor of the garlic butter.

- **Storage:** Leftover cheesy garlic bread can be stored in an airtight container in the refrigerator for up to 2 days. Reheat in the oven or toaster oven to maintain crispiness before serving.

Cheesy garlic bread is a crowd-pleasing treat that's perfect for sharing with family and friends. Enjoy its buttery, garlicky goodness alongside your favorite meals or as a tasty snack!

Creamy Peanut Butter Fudge

Ingredients:

- 1 cup creamy peanut butter
- 1 cup unsalted butter
- 1 teaspoon vanilla extract
- 4 cups powdered sugar (confectioners' sugar)
- Optional: 1/4 cup chopped peanuts (for added texture)

Instructions:

1. **Prepare the pan:**
    - Line an 8x8 inch (20x20 cm) baking dish with parchment paper or foil. Leave an overhang on the sides for easy removal of the fudge later.
2. **Melt the butter:**
    - In a medium saucepan, melt the unsalted butter over medium heat. Stir occasionally until completely melted and smooth.
3. **Add peanut butter and vanilla:**
    - Stir in the creamy peanut butter and vanilla extract into the melted butter until well combined and smooth.
4. **Incorporate powdered sugar:**
    - Remove the saucepan from heat. Gradually add the powdered sugar, 1 cup at a time, stirring well after each addition until the mixture is smooth and thick. It will resemble a thick dough.
5. **Optional: Add chopped peanuts:**
    - If desired, stir in chopped peanuts to add a crunchy texture to the fudge mixture.
6. **Transfer to the pan:**
    - Spread the peanut butter fudge mixture evenly into the prepared baking dish. Use a spatula or the back of a spoon to smooth the top.
7. **Chill the fudge:**
    - Refrigerate the fudge for at least 2 hours, or until firm and set.
8. **Cut and serve:**
    - Once the fudge is firm, lift it out of the baking dish using the parchment paper or foil overhang. Place it on a cutting board and cut into squares or rectangles.
9. **Store:**
    - Store the creamy peanut butter fudge in an airtight container in the refrigerator for up to 2 weeks. For longer storage, you can freeze the fudge for up to 2 months.

Tips:

- **Variations:** You can customize your creamy peanut butter fudge by adding chocolate chips, swirling in melted chocolate on top, or sprinkling sea salt for a sweet and salty flavor.

- **Softening powdered sugar:** If your powdered sugar is clumpy, sift it before adding it to the mixture to ensure a smooth consistency.
- **Room temperature ingredients:** For easier mixing, ensure the peanut butter and butter are at room temperature before starting the recipe.

Creamy peanut butter fudge is a delicious treat that's perfect for holidays, parties, or as a homemade gift. Enjoy the creamy texture and rich peanut butter flavor with every bite!

Cream Cheese Stuffed Bell Peppers

Ingredients:

- 4 large bell peppers (any color)
- 8 oz (225g) cream cheese, softened
- 1 cup shredded cheddar cheese (or cheese of your choice)
- 1/2 cup grated Parmesan cheese
- 1/2 teaspoon garlic powder
- 1/2 teaspoon onion powder
- 1/4 teaspoon paprika
- Salt and pepper, to taste
- Fresh herbs, such as parsley or chives, chopped (optional, for garnish)

Instructions:

1. **Preheat the oven:**
   - Preheat your oven to 375°F (190°C). Grease a baking dish large enough to hold the bell peppers upright.
2. **Prepare the bell peppers:**
   - Cut the tops off the bell peppers and remove the seeds and membranes from inside. Rinse the peppers under cold water and pat dry with paper towels.
3. **Make the cream cheese filling:**
   - In a mixing bowl, combine the softened cream cheese, shredded cheddar cheese, grated Parmesan cheese, garlic powder, onion powder, paprika, salt, and pepper. Mix until smooth and well combined.
4. **Stuff the bell peppers:**
   - Spoon the cream cheese mixture evenly into each bell pepper until they are filled to the top. You can press the filling down gently to compact it.
5. **Bake the stuffed peppers:**
   - Place the stuffed bell peppers upright in the prepared baking dish. Cover the dish with foil and bake in the preheated oven for 25-30 minutes.
6. **Optional: Add topping and finish baking:**
   - Remove the foil from the baking dish and continue baking for an additional 10-15 minutes, or until the peppers are tender and the cheese is melted and lightly golden on top.
7. **Garnish and serve:**
   - Remove the stuffed bell peppers from the oven and let them cool slightly before serving.
   - Garnish with chopped fresh herbs like parsley or chives, if desired.

Tips:

- **Variations:** You can add cooked ground meat (such as sausage or ground beef) or vegetables (such as spinach or mushrooms) to the cream cheese mixture for added flavor and texture.
- **Make-ahead:** Prepare the cream cheese filling and stuff the bell peppers in advance. Cover and refrigerate until ready to bake. Allow a few extra minutes of baking time if baking directly from the refrigerator.
- **Serve:** Cream cheese stuffed bell peppers can be served as a side dish or appetizer. They pair well with a side salad or roasted vegetables.

Cream cheese stuffed bell peppers are a flavorful and satisfying dish that's perfect for any occasion. Enjoy the creamy filling and the sweetness of the roasted bell peppers with every bite!

Bacon-Wrapped Filet Mignon

Ingredients:

- 4 filet mignon steaks, about 6-8 oz each and 1 1/2 inches thick
- 8 slices of bacon, preferably thick-cut
- Salt and freshly ground black pepper, to taste
- Olive oil, for cooking
- Optional: Garlic powder, onion powder, or steak seasoning for additional flavor

Instructions:

1. **Preheat the oven:**
    - Preheat your oven to 400°F (200°C).
2. **Wrap the filet mignon with bacon:**
    - Season each filet mignon steak with salt, freshly ground black pepper, and any additional seasonings you prefer (such as garlic powder or steak seasoning).
    - Wrap each steak with 2 slices of bacon, securing the ends with toothpicks to hold the bacon in place. Make sure the bacon covers the sides of the steak.
3. **Sear the steaks:**
    - Heat a large oven-safe skillet or cast iron pan over medium-high heat. Add a drizzle of olive oil to coat the bottom of the pan.
    - Carefully place the bacon-wrapped filet mignon steaks in the hot skillet. Sear for 2-3 minutes on each side, including the edges, until the bacon is browned and crispy.
4. **Transfer to the oven:**
    - Transfer the skillet with the seared filet mignon steaks to the preheated oven.
    - Roast in the oven for about 10-12 minutes for medium-rare doneness (or adjust cooking time according to your preferred level of doneness).
5. **Rest and serve:**
    - Remove the bacon-wrapped filet mignon from the oven and transfer them to a plate or cutting board. Remove the toothpicks.
    - Let the steaks rest for 5-10 minutes before serving to allow the juices to redistribute.
6. **Optional: Serve with sauce or side dishes:**
    - Serve the bacon-wrapped filet mignon steaks on their own or with your favorite sauce (such as peppercorn sauce or garlic butter).
    - Pair with sides like mashed potatoes, roasted vegetables, or a crisp salad.

Tips:

- **Quality of ingredients:** Use high-quality, thick-cut bacon and well-marbled filet mignon steaks for best results.
- **Oven temperature:** Cooking times may vary depending on the thickness of the filet mignon and your desired level of doneness. Use a meat thermometer to check for an

internal temperature of 130-135°F (54-57°C) for medium-rare, 140°F (60°C) for medium, or adjust accordingly.
- **Alternative cooking method:** If you prefer, you can also grill the bacon-wrapped filet mignon over medium-high heat on a preheated grill until the bacon is crispy and the steaks reach your desired level of doneness.

Bacon-wrapped filet mignon is a decadent and flavorful dish that's perfect for special occasions or a gourmet dinner at home. Enjoy the combination of tender steak and crispy bacon for a memorable meal!

Cheesy Broccoli Casserole

Ingredients:

- 4 cups broccoli florets, fresh or frozen
- 1 cup shredded cheddar cheese
- 1/2 cup shredded mozzarella cheese
- 1/2 cup mayonnaise
- 1/2 cup sour cream
- 1/4 cup grated Parmesan cheese
- 1/2 teaspoon garlic powder
- Salt and pepper, to taste
- Optional: 1/4 cup chopped onion or 2 cloves garlic, minced
- Optional: 1/2 cup crushed buttery crackers or breadcrumbs for topping

Instructions:

1. **Preheat the oven:**
   - Preheat your oven to 350°F (175°C). Grease a 9x9 inch (23x23 cm) baking dish with butter or cooking spray.
2. **Prepare the broccoli:**
   - If using fresh broccoli, blanch the broccoli florets in boiling water for 2-3 minutes until slightly tender. Drain well. If using frozen broccoli, thaw and drain any excess water.
3. **Make the cheese sauce:**
   - In a large bowl, combine the shredded cheddar cheese, shredded mozzarella cheese, mayonnaise, sour cream, grated Parmesan cheese, garlic powder, salt, and pepper. Add chopped onion or minced garlic if using.
4. **Combine broccoli and cheese sauce:**
   - Add the blanched or thawed broccoli florets to the cheese sauce mixture. Stir gently to coat the broccoli evenly with the sauce.
5. **Transfer to baking dish:**
   - Transfer the broccoli mixture to the prepared baking dish, spreading it out evenly.
6. **Optional: Add topping:**
   - If desired, sprinkle crushed buttery crackers or breadcrumbs evenly over the top of the casserole for added crunch.
7. **Bake the casserole:**
   - Cover the baking dish with foil and bake in the preheated oven for 20-25 minutes.
   - Remove the foil and bake for an additional 10-15 minutes, or until the cheese is melted and bubbly, and the top is golden brown.
8. **Serve:**
   - Remove the cheesy broccoli casserole from the oven and let it cool slightly before serving.
   - Serve warm as a side dish or a main dish.

Tips:

- **Variations:** Feel free to add cooked and diced chicken, ham, or bacon to make it a heartier main dish.
- **Storage:** Leftover cheesy broccoli casserole can be stored in an airtight container in the refrigerator for up to 3 days. Reheat in the oven or microwave until warmed through before serving.
- **Creamy consistency:** For a creamier texture, you can add a splash of milk or cream to the cheese sauce mixture.

Cheesy broccoli casserole is a crowd-pleasing dish that's perfect for potlucks, holiday gatherings, or a cozy family dinner. Enjoy the creamy cheese sauce and tender broccoli in every bite!

Buttered Popcorn with Sea Salt

Ingredients:

- 1/2 cup popcorn kernels
- 2-3 tablespoons unsalted butter, melted
- Sea salt, to taste

Instructions:

1. **Pop the popcorn:**
   - Heat a large pot or a stovetop popcorn popper over medium heat. Add a small amount of vegetable oil (about 2 tablespoons) to the pot and swirl it around to coat the bottom evenly.
   - Add the popcorn kernels to the pot in a single layer. Cover with a lid.
2. **Pop the popcorn:**
   - Shake the pot occasionally to ensure even heating. The kernels will begin to pop. Continue shaking gently until the popping slows down, about 2-3 minutes. Remove from heat.
3. **Melt the butter:**
   - While the popcorn is popping, melt the unsalted butter in a microwave-safe bowl or small saucepan until fully melted.
4. **Combine popcorn and butter:**
   - Transfer the popped popcorn to a large bowl. Drizzle the melted butter over the popcorn, tossing the popcorn gently with a spoon or spatula to evenly coat.
5. **Season with sea salt:**
   - Sprinkle sea salt over the buttered popcorn, adjusting the amount to your taste preference. Toss the popcorn again to distribute the salt evenly.
6. **Serve immediately:**
   - Enjoy the buttered popcorn with sea salt while it's still warm and freshly seasoned.

Tips:

- **Variations:** For added flavor, you can sprinkle other seasonings such as grated Parmesan cheese, nutritional yeast, smoked paprika, or garlic powder over the buttered popcorn.
- **Air-popped popcorn:** If you prefer a healthier option, you can use an air popper to pop the popcorn kernels instead of using oil on the stovetop.
- **Storage:** Store any leftover buttered popcorn in an airtight container or resealable bag at room temperature. It's best enjoyed fresh, but you can reheat it in the oven or microwave for a short time to restore crispness.

Buttered popcorn with sea salt is a classic snack that's perfect for movie nights, gatherings, or anytime you're craving a savory treat. Enjoy the simple pleasure of homemade popcorn with this easy recipe!

Keto Cheese Crackers

Ingredients:

- 1 1/2 cups shredded mozzarella cheese
- 2 oz (about 1/2 cup) grated Parmesan cheese
- 2 oz (about 1/2 cup) almond flour
- 2 tablespoons cream cheese, softened
- 1 large egg
- 1/2 teaspoon garlic powder
- 1/2 teaspoon onion powder
- 1/2 teaspoon dried Italian herbs (optional)
- Salt and pepper, to taste
- Sesame seeds, poppy seeds, or flaky sea salt (optional, for topping)

Instructions:

1. **Preheat the oven:**
   - Preheat your oven to 350°F (175°C). Line a baking sheet with parchment paper.
2. **Prepare the dough:**
   - In a microwave-safe bowl, combine the shredded mozzarella cheese and cream cheese. Microwave in 30-second intervals, stirring in between, until the cheese is melted and smooth.
3. **Add remaining ingredients:**
   - To the melted cheese mixture, add the grated Parmesan cheese, almond flour, egg, garlic powder, onion powder, dried herbs (if using), salt, and pepper. Mix until a dough forms. If the dough is too sticky, you can chill it in the refrigerator for 10-15 minutes.
4. **Roll out the dough:**
   - Place the dough between two sheets of parchment paper. Use a rolling pin to roll out the dough into a thin, even layer (about 1/8 inch thick).
5. **Cut into crackers:**
   - Use a pizza cutter or knife to cut the rolled-out dough into small squares or rectangles, about 1 inch in size.
6. **Top with seeds or salt (optional):**
   - If desired, sprinkle sesame seeds, poppy seeds, or flaky sea salt over the tops of the crackers for added flavor and texture.
7. **Bake the crackers:**
   - Transfer the parchment paper with the cut crackers to the baking sheet. Bake in the preheated oven for 10-12 minutes, or until the crackers are golden brown and crispy.
8. **Cool and serve:**
   - Remove the baking sheet from the oven and let the crackers cool on the sheet for a few minutes. Then transfer them to a wire rack to cool completely and crisp up.

9. **Store:**
    - Store the keto cheese crackers in an airtight container at room temperature for up to 1 week. You can also freeze them for longer storage.

Tips:

- **Variations:** Experiment with different cheeses such as cheddar or Gouda for different flavors of keto crackers.
- **Flavorings:** Customize the flavor of your keto cheese crackers by adding herbs like rosemary, thyme, or paprika to the dough.
- **Serve with:** Enjoy these keto cheese crackers on their own, with dips like guacamole or cream cheese, or alongside soups and salads.

These keto cheese crackers are crispy, flavorful, and perfect for satisfying your crunchy snack cravings while sticking to your low-carb diet. Enjoy the cheesy goodness without the guilt of carbs!

Creamy Avocado Soup with Bacon

Ingredients:

- 4 ripe avocados, peeled, pitted, and diced
- 6 slices of bacon, chopped
- 1 small onion, diced
- 2 cloves garlic, minced
- 4 cups chicken or vegetable broth
- 1/2 cup heavy cream or coconut cream (for a dairy-free option)
- 2 tablespoons lime juice (about 1 lime)
- Salt and pepper, to taste
- Optional garnishes: chopped fresh cilantro, diced tomatoes, sour cream, or shredded cheese

Instructions:

1. **Cook the bacon:**
    - In a large pot or Dutch oven, cook the chopped bacon over medium heat until crispy. Remove the bacon with a slotted spoon and set aside on a plate lined with paper towels to drain excess grease. Leave about 1 tablespoon of bacon grease in the pot.
2. **Sauté onion and garlic:**
    - In the same pot with the bacon grease, sauté the diced onion until softened and translucent, about 3-4 minutes. Add the minced garlic and cook for an additional 1 minute until fragrant.
3. **Add avocados and broth:**
    - Add the diced avocados to the pot with the sautéed onion and garlic. Pour in the chicken or vegetable broth, stirring to combine. Bring to a simmer over medium heat.
4. **Simmer and blend:**
    - Reduce the heat to low and let the soup simmer for about 10 minutes, allowing the flavors to meld together. Remove the pot from the heat.
    - Use an immersion blender to blend the soup until smooth and creamy. Alternatively, transfer the soup in batches to a blender and blend until smooth. Be cautious when blending hot liquids.
5. **Add cream and lime juice:**
    - Stir in the heavy cream or coconut cream (for dairy-free option) and lime juice. Season with salt and pepper to taste. Adjust the consistency with additional broth if needed.
6. **Serve:**
    - Ladle the creamy avocado soup into bowls. Top each serving with a generous sprinkling of crispy bacon pieces and any optional garnishes you prefer, such as chopped fresh cilantro, diced tomatoes, sour cream, or shredded cheese.
7. **Enjoy:**

- Serve the creamy avocado soup with bacon immediately while warm. Enjoy the creamy texture of the avocado soup balanced with the savory crunch of bacon.

Tips:

- **Avocado ripeness:** Use ripe avocados for the best creamy texture. They should yield slightly to gentle pressure when squeezed.
- **Make it ahead:** This soup can be made ahead of time and stored in the refrigerator for up to 2 days. Reheat gently on the stove before serving.
- **Variations:** For added flavor, you can incorporate spices like cumin, paprika, or chili powder to the soup base.

Creamy avocado soup with bacon is a comforting and flavorful dish that's perfect for lunch or dinner. Enjoy its creamy goodness and rich flavors with every spoonful!

Cheesy Mashed Potatoes

Ingredients:

- 2 lbs (about 900g) potatoes (such as Russet or Yukon Gold), peeled and cut into chunks
- 1/2 cup milk (preferably whole milk or half-and-half), warmed
- 1/4 cup unsalted butter, cut into cubes
- 1 cup shredded cheddar cheese (or cheese of your choice)
- Salt and pepper, to taste
- Optional: Chopped fresh chives or parsley for garnish

Instructions:

1. **Cook the potatoes:**
   - Place the peeled and chopped potatoes in a large pot and cover with cold water. Add a generous pinch of salt.
   - Bring the water to a boil over medium-high heat. Reduce the heat to medium-low and simmer the potatoes for 15-20 minutes, or until they are fork-tender and easily pierced with a knife.
2. **Prepare the cheese mixture:**
   - While the potatoes are cooking, warm the milk in a small saucepan over low heat or in the microwave until it's warm to the touch (not boiling).
   - In a separate bowl, combine the shredded cheddar cheese and cubed unsalted butter.
3. **Mash the potatoes:**
   - Drain the cooked potatoes well and return them to the pot. Use a potato masher or a fork to mash the potatoes until smooth and lump-free.
4. **Add cheese and milk:**
   - Gradually add the warmed milk to the mashed potatoes, stirring continuously, until the potatoes reach your desired creamy consistency.
   - Fold in the cheese and butter mixture until the cheese is melted and well combined with the potatoes. Season with salt and pepper to taste.
5. **Serve:**
   - Transfer the cheesy mashed potatoes to a serving bowl. Garnish with chopped fresh chives or parsley, if desired.
   - Serve hot as a side dish with your favorite main course.

Tips:

- **Variations:** Experiment with different types of cheese, such as Gouda, Parmesan, or a blend of cheeses, to customize the flavor of your mashed potatoes.
- **Creaminess:** For extra creamy mashed potatoes, you can use more butter and milk according to your preference.

- **Make ahead:** You can prepare the mashed potatoes ahead of time and reheat them gently on the stove or in the microwave. Add a splash of milk if needed to restore creaminess.

Cheesy mashed potatoes are a comforting addition to any meal, whether it's a holiday feast or a weeknight dinner. Enjoy the creamy texture and cheesy goodness with this easy and satisfying recipe!

Creamy Caesar Salad with Bacon Bits

Ingredients:

For the salad:

- 1 head of romaine lettuce, washed and chopped
- 1 cup cherry tomatoes, halved
- 1/4 cup grated Parmesan cheese
- 1/4 cup bacon bits (cooked and crumbled)
- Optional: Croutons (homemade or store-bought)

For the creamy Caesar dressing:

- 1/2 cup mayonnaise
- 1/4 cup grated Parmesan cheese
- 2 tablespoons freshly squeezed lemon juice
- 1 tablespoon Dijon mustard
- 1-2 garlic cloves, minced
- 1/2 teaspoon Worcestershire sauce
- Salt and pepper, to taste
- 2-4 tablespoons water, to thin the dressing (if needed)

Instructions:

1. **Prepare the creamy Caesar dressing:**
   - In a bowl, whisk together mayonnaise, grated Parmesan cheese, lemon juice, Dijon mustard, minced garlic, Worcestershire sauce, salt, and pepper.
   - If the dressing is too thick, add water, 1 tablespoon at a time, until you reach the desired consistency. Taste and adjust seasoning as needed.
2. **Assemble the salad:**
   - In a large salad bowl, combine chopped romaine lettuce, cherry tomatoes, grated Parmesan cheese, and bacon bits.
   - Optionally, add croutons for extra crunch.
3. **Toss with the dressing:**
   - Pour the creamy Caesar dressing over the salad ingredients. Toss gently until everything is evenly coated with the dressing.
4. **Serve:**
   - Divide the salad among individual serving plates or bowls.
   - Garnish with additional bacon bits and grated Parmesan cheese, if desired.
5. **Enjoy:**
   - Serve the creamy Caesar salad with bacon bits immediately as a delicious side dish or add grilled chicken or shrimp to turn it into a main course.

Tips:

- **Make ahead:** You can prepare the creamy Caesar dressing and store it in the refrigerator for up to 3 days. Shake or whisk well before using.
- **Variations:** Add grilled chicken or shrimp for a protein-packed version of this salad. You can also sprinkle with additional toppings like sliced avocado or hard-boiled eggs.
- **Homemade bacon bits:** Cook bacon until crispy, then crumble it into small pieces for fresh and flavorful bacon bits.

Creamy Caesar salad with bacon bits is a crowd-pleasing dish that's perfect for any occasion, from weeknight dinners to gatherings and parties. Enjoy the creamy dressing paired with the savory crunch of bacon in every bite!

Buttered Corn on the Cob

Ingredients:

- Fresh corn on the cob, husked
- Butter, softened (about 1 tablespoon per ear of corn)
- Salt, to taste
- Optional: Freshly ground black pepper, chopped herbs (such as parsley or chives)

Instructions:

1. **Prepare the corn:**
   - Peel back the husks of the corn, remove the silk (the stringy part), and then pull the husks back over the corn.
2. **Cook the corn:**
   - Bring a large pot of water to a boil. Add the prepared corn and cook for 5-7 minutes, or until the corn is tender and easily pierced with a fork.
3. **Butter the corn:**
   - Remove the corn from the boiling water and let it cool slightly until it's comfortable to handle.
   - Peel back the husks and discard them. Spread butter evenly over each ear of corn while it's still warm. The residual heat will help melt the butter and spread it evenly.
4. **Season and serve:**
   - Sprinkle salt over the buttered corn to taste. Optionally, add freshly ground black pepper and chopped herbs for additional flavor.
5. **Enjoy:**
   - Serve the buttered corn on the cob immediately while it's warm and freshly buttered.

Tips:

- **Grilled corn:** For added flavor, you can grill the corn on a hot grill instead of boiling it. Brush the corn with butter while grilling for a smoky, grilled flavor.
- **Variations:** Experiment with different flavored butters, such as garlic butter or herb butter, for a twist on traditional buttered corn.
- **Storage:** Buttered corn on the cob is best enjoyed fresh, but if you have leftovers, you can store them in the refrigerator in an airtight container for up to 2 days. Reheat gently in the microwave or on the stovetop with a little extra butter.

Buttered corn on the cob is a simple and tasty way to enjoy fresh corn, highlighting its natural sweetness with a rich, buttery finish. It's a versatile side dish that complements a wide range of meals!

Keto Chocolate Mousse

Ingredients:

- 4 oz (about 115g) unsweetened chocolate, chopped
- 1/4 cup unsalted butter
- 1/4 cup powdered erythritol or your preferred keto-friendly sweetener
- 1 teaspoon vanilla extract
- 1 cup heavy cream
- Optional: Whipped cream and cocoa powder for garnish

Instructions:

1. **Melt chocolate and butter:**
   - In a heatproof bowl, combine the chopped unsweetened chocolate and unsalted butter. Melt them together using a double boiler or in short bursts in the microwave, stirring frequently until smooth and fully melted.
2. **Sweeten and flavor:**
   - Stir in the powdered erythritol (or sweetener of your choice) and vanilla extract into the melted chocolate mixture. Mix until well combined. Taste and adjust sweetness if needed.
3. **Whip the cream:**
   - In a separate bowl, whip the heavy cream until stiff peaks form. Be careful not to over-whip; you want a smooth and creamy texture.
4. **Combine and chill:**
   - Gently fold the whipped cream into the chocolate mixture in batches. Fold until no streaks remain and the mousse is smooth and well incorporated.
5. **Chill:**
   - Transfer the keto chocolate mousse into serving glasses or bowls. Cover with plastic wrap and refrigerate for at least 1-2 hours, or until the mousse is set.
6. **Serve:**
   - Before serving, garnish with a dollop of whipped cream and a dusting of cocoa powder if desired.

Tips:

- **Chocolate selection:** Use high-quality unsweetened chocolate with a cocoa content of around 70% or higher for the best flavor.
- **Sweetener:** Adjust the amount of sweetener to your taste preferences. Some keto-friendly sweeteners are sweeter than others, so taste and adjust accordingly.
- **Storage:** Store any leftover keto chocolate mousse in the refrigerator, covered, for up to 3-4 days.

Keto chocolate mousse is a rich and satisfying dessert that's perfect for those following a low-carb or keto diet. Enjoy its creamy texture and intense chocolate flavor without the guilt of added sugars!

Brie and Bacon Stuffed Chicken Thighs

Ingredients:

- 4 boneless, skinless chicken thighs
- Salt and pepper, to taste
- 4 slices of bacon, cooked until crispy and crumbled
- 4 oz brie cheese, thinly sliced
- 2 tablespoons olive oil
- 1 teaspoon garlic powder
- 1 teaspoon paprika
- Fresh thyme or parsley, chopped (for garnish)

Instructions:

1. **Prepare the chicken thighs:**
    - Preheat your oven to 375°F (190°C).
    - Season both sides of the chicken thighs with salt and pepper.
2. **Stuff the chicken thighs:**
    - Lay the chicken thighs flat on a cutting board. Place a few slices of brie cheese and a portion of the crumbled bacon in the center of each thigh.
3. **Roll and secure:**
    - Roll up each chicken thigh tightly around the filling, and secure with toothpicks to hold them together.
4. **Season and sear:**
    - In a large oven-safe skillet or frying pan, heat olive oil over medium-high heat.
    - Sprinkle garlic powder and paprika over the rolled chicken thighs. Sear the chicken thighs on all sides until golden brown, about 2-3 minutes per side.
5. **Bake:**
    - Transfer the skillet with the seared chicken thighs to the preheated oven.
    - Bake for 20-25 minutes, or until the chicken thighs are cooked through and reach an internal temperature of 165°F (74°C).
6. **Rest and serve:**
    - Remove the chicken thighs from the oven and let them rest for a few minutes.
    - Remove the toothpicks carefully before serving.
    - Garnish with chopped fresh thyme or parsley.
7. **Serve:**
    - Serve the brie and bacon stuffed chicken thighs hot, accompanied by your favorite side dishes like roasted vegetables or a fresh salad.

Tips:

- **Variations:** Feel free to add spinach or sun-dried tomatoes to the stuffing for extra flavor and texture.

- **Cheese options:** If you prefer a different type of cheese, such as goat cheese or gouda, you can substitute it for the brie.
- **Side dishes:** This dish pairs well with a variety of sides, including mashed potatoes, steamed green beans, or cauliflower rice.

Brie and bacon stuffed chicken thighs make for an elegant yet straightforward dish that's sure to impress with its creamy, savory flavors. Enjoy this delicious meal for a special dinner or any time you want a comforting and satisfying meal!

Creamy Coleslaw with Mayonnaise

Ingredients:

- 1 small head of green cabbage, finely shredded (about 4 cups)
- 1 large carrot, grated
- 1/2 cup mayonnaise
- 2 tablespoons apple cider vinegar (or white vinegar)
- 1 tablespoon Dijon mustard
- 1-2 tablespoons granulated sugar, or to taste (optional)
- Salt and pepper, to taste

Instructions:

1. **Prepare the vegetables:**
   - Finely shred the green cabbage using a sharp knife or a mandoline slicer. Grate the carrot using a box grater or a food processor fitted with a grating attachment.
2. **Make the dressing:**
   - In a large mixing bowl, whisk together the mayonnaise, apple cider vinegar, Dijon mustard, and optional sugar until smooth and well combined.
3. **Combine the coleslaw:**
   - Add the shredded cabbage and grated carrot to the bowl with the dressing.
   - Toss the vegetables with the dressing until they are evenly coated. Use a spoon or tongs to mix well.
4. **Season and chill:**
   - Season the coleslaw with salt and pepper to taste. Adjust the seasoning and sweetness (if using sugar) according to your preferences.
   - Cover the bowl with plastic wrap or transfer the coleslaw to an airtight container. Refrigerate for at least 1 hour before serving to allow the flavors to meld together and the coleslaw to chill.
5. **Serve:**
   - Before serving, give the coleslaw a final toss to ensure the dressing is evenly distributed.
   - Serve the creamy coleslaw as a side dish alongside grilled meats, sandwiches, burgers, or as a topping for tacos and wraps.

Tips:

- **Variations:** Customize your coleslaw by adding sliced green onions, chopped fresh herbs (such as parsley or dill), or a handful of raisins or dried cranberries for a touch of sweetness.
- **Make ahead:** Creamy coleslaw can be made ahead of time and stored in the refrigerator for up to 2-3 days. Stir well before serving.
- **Creaminess:** For a richer coleslaw, you can increase the amount of mayonnaise or add a tablespoon of sour cream or Greek yogurt to the dressing.

Creamy coleslaw with mayonnaise is a refreshing and satisfying side dish that's perfect for picnics, barbecues, and everyday meals. Enjoy its crunchy texture and creamy dressing that complements a wide range of dishes!

Cheesesteak Stuffed Peppers

Ingredients:

- 4 large bell peppers (any color), halved lengthwise and seeds removed
- 1 lb (450g) thinly sliced steak (such as ribeye or sirloin)
- 1 large onion, thinly sliced
- 1 green bell pepper, thinly sliced
- 8 slices provolone cheese
- 2 tablespoons olive oil
- Salt and pepper, to taste
- Optional: Sliced mushrooms, chopped garlic, hot sauce for serving

Instructions:

1. **Prepare the bell peppers:**
    - Preheat your oven to 375°F (190°C).
    - Cut the bell peppers in half lengthwise and remove the seeds and membranes. Place the pepper halves cut-side up on a baking sheet lined with parchment paper or aluminum foil.
2. **Cook the steak and vegetables:**
    - In a large skillet, heat 1 tablespoon of olive oil over medium-high heat. Add the thinly sliced steak and cook until browned and cooked through, about 3-4 minutes per side. Season with salt and pepper to taste. Remove the steak from the skillet and set aside.
    - In the same skillet, add another tablespoon of olive oil if needed. Add the sliced onion and green bell pepper. Cook until the vegetables are tender and caramelized, about 5-7 minutes. Season with salt and pepper.
3. **Assemble the stuffed peppers:**
    - Place a slice of provolone cheese at the bottom of each bell pepper half.
    - Divide the cooked steak evenly among the bell pepper halves, filling each one.
    - Top each bell pepper half with the sautéed onion and green pepper mixture.
4. **Bake:**
    - Place the baking sheet with the stuffed peppers in the preheated oven.
    - Bake for 15-20 minutes, or until the bell peppers are tender and the cheese is melted and bubbly.
5. **Serve:**
    - Remove the stuffed peppers from the oven and let them cool slightly before serving.
    - Optionally, garnish with chopped parsley and serve with hot sauce on the side.

Tips:

- **Cheese variation:** Feel free to use your favorite cheese, such as cheddar or mozzarella, instead of provolone.

- **Additional toppings:** Customize your cheesesteak stuffed peppers with sliced mushrooms, chopped garlic, or your favorite hot sauce for added flavor.
- **Make ahead:** You can prepare the filling ahead of time and store it in an airtight container in the refrigerator. Assemble and bake the stuffed peppers when ready to serve.

Cheesesteak stuffed peppers are a satisfying and flavorful meal that's perfect for a low-carb dinner option. Enjoy the savory steak, melted cheese, and sweet bell peppers in every bite!

Creamy Pumpkin Soup with Coconut Milk

Ingredients:

- 2 tablespoons olive oil or coconut oil
- 1 onion, chopped
- 3 cloves garlic, minced
- 1 teaspoon grated ginger (optional)
- 1 teaspoon ground cumin
- 1/2 teaspoon ground coriander
- 1/2 teaspoon ground cinnamon
- 1/4 teaspoon ground nutmeg
- 1/4 teaspoon cayenne pepper (adjust to taste)
- 4 cups pumpkin puree (canned or homemade)
- 4 cups vegetable broth or chicken broth
- 1 can (13.5 oz) full-fat coconut milk
- Salt and pepper, to taste
- Optional toppings: Toasted pumpkin seeds, a drizzle of coconut milk, chopped fresh herbs (such as parsley or cilantro)

Instructions:

1. **Sauté aromatics:**
   - Heat olive oil or coconut oil in a large pot over medium heat. Add chopped onion and sauté until softened and translucent, about 5-7 minutes.
   - Add minced garlic and grated ginger (if using), and sauté for another 1-2 minutes until fragrant.
2. **Add spices:**
   - Stir in ground cumin, ground coriander, ground cinnamon, ground nutmeg, and cayenne pepper. Cook for 1 minute until spices are toasted and fragrant.
3. **Simmer with pumpkin and broth:**
   - Add pumpkin puree to the pot and stir to combine with the aromatics and spices.
   - Pour in vegetable broth or chicken broth, stirring well. Bring the mixture to a boil, then reduce the heat to low and let it simmer for about 15-20 minutes to allow the flavors to meld together.
4. **Blend the soup:**
   - Using an immersion blender directly in the pot, blend the soup until smooth and creamy. Alternatively, carefully transfer the soup in batches to a blender and blend until smooth. Be cautious with hot liquids.
5. **Add coconut milk:**
   - Stir in the can of coconut milk, reserving a small amount for garnish if desired. Simmer the soup for an additional 5 minutes to heat through and blend flavors.
6. **Season and serve:**
   - Season the creamy pumpkin soup with salt and pepper to taste. Adjust spices if needed.

- Ladle the soup into bowls and garnish with toasted pumpkin seeds, a drizzle of coconut milk, and chopped fresh herbs.

Tips:

- **Pumpkin puree:** You can use canned pumpkin puree or homemade roasted pumpkin puree for this recipe.
- **Consistency:** Adjust the consistency of the soup by adding more broth if it's too thick, or simmering longer if it's too thin.
- **Make ahead:** This soup can be made ahead of time and stored in the refrigerator for up to 3-4 days. Reheat gently on the stove before serving.

Creamy pumpkin soup with coconut milk is a comforting and nourishing dish that's perfect for autumn or winter. Enjoy its creamy texture and warm spices as a starter or a light meal paired with crusty bread or a salad!

Keto Cheesecake Fat Bombs

Ingredients:

- 8 oz cream cheese, softened
- 4 tablespoons unsalted butter, softened
- 1/4 cup powdered erythritol or your preferred keto-friendly sweetener
- 1 teaspoon vanilla extract
- 1/4 cup coconut flour
- Optional: Sugar-free chocolate chips or chopped nuts for coating (if desired)

Instructions:

1. **Mix the base ingredients:**
   - In a mixing bowl, combine softened cream cheese and butter. Use a hand mixer or stand mixer to beat until smooth and creamy.
2. **Sweeten and flavor:**
   - Add powdered erythritol (or sweetener of choice) and vanilla extract to the cream cheese mixture. Beat again until well combined.
3. **Add coconut flour:**
   - Gradually add coconut flour to the mixture, stirring until thoroughly incorporated. The mixture should be thick enough to roll into balls.
4. **Shape the fat bombs:**
   - Line a baking sheet with parchment paper. Using a spoon or a small cookie scoop, portion out the cheesecake mixture and roll into balls about 1 inch in diameter. Place them on the lined baking sheet.
5. **Optional coating:**
   - If desired, roll each fat bomb in sugar-free chocolate chips or chopped nuts to coat. This step adds texture and additional flavor.
6. **Chill and store:**
   - Place the baking sheet with the fat bombs in the refrigerator to chill for at least 1 hour, or until firm.
7. **Serve and enjoy:**
   - Once chilled and firm, transfer the fat bombs to an airtight container. Store in the refrigerator until ready to serve.

Tips:

- **Variations:** Experiment with different flavors by adding lemon zest or cocoa powder to the cheesecake mixture.
- **Storage:** Keep the fat bombs refrigerated in an airtight container for up to 1 week. They can also be frozen for longer storage.
- **Portion control:** These fat bombs are rich and satisfying, so one or two can be a satisfying treat without overindulging in carbs.

Keto cheesecake fat bombs are a delightful way to satisfy your sweet cravings while staying within your low-carb goals. Enjoy them as a snack or dessert anytime you need a little something extra!